LOVE and BEADS

CONTENTS

Flower Ring & Earrings, Twisted Necklace

The combination of pearl and crystal beads in subdued colors gives these pieces a serene, elegant look.

Instructions are on pp. 38-39.

Black Green Topaz Aurora Pink

Pearl & Crystal Bracelet

This marriage of Swarovski pearl and crystal beads creates a radiant luster.
Instructions are on p. 37.

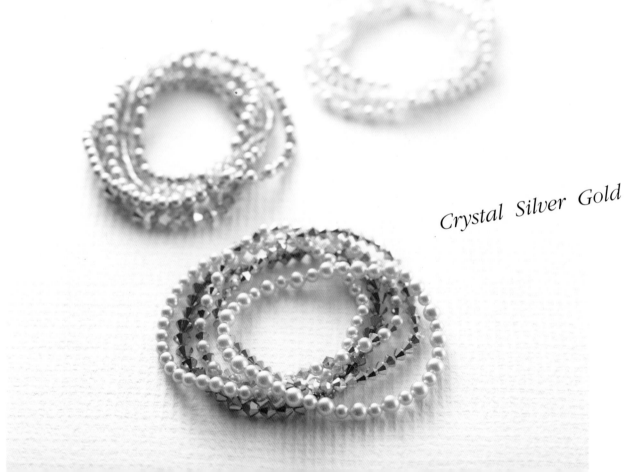

Crystal Silver Gold

Pearl & Crystal Flower Ring
Pearl Choker & Earrings

The same technique is used to make the choker pictured on this page and the choker with leather cord shown on p. 51. For a truly regal effect, wear it with the matching earrings and the flower ring.

Instructions for flower ring are on p. 38.   Instructions for choker and earrings are on p. 40.

Heart Necklace

This beautiful, must-have necklace with its heart center
is crafted from 3-mm Swarovski crystals.

Instructions are on pp. 58-60

Heart Ring

You'll want to make this lovely ring in every color.
IInstructions are on pp. 60-61.

Red White Pink Blue Light blue

Venetian Glass Bead Necklace

Pastel Venetian glass beads and crackled glass bead
accents add up to a very stylish necklace.
Instructions are on p. 41.

Venetian Glass
Bead Earrings

These simple but chic earrings feature Venetian glass beads.
Instructions are on p. 41.

Pink Blue

Snowflake Choker & Earrings

You'll look dazzling when you wear these pieces with their ever-popular snowflake motifs.

Instructions are on pp. 42-43.

Silver Crystal

Choker & Bracelet with Floral Motif

These geometric pieces are made even more striking by the crystal-bead accents on the floral motifs.

Instructions are on p. 43.

Disk Bead Ring, Earrings & Necklace

Disc and bugle beads grace the lustrous ring, earrings and necklace shown on this page.
Instructions are on pp. 44-45 (instructions for earrings not included).

Bugle Bead Bracelet

This bracelet, featuring translucent bugle beads, enhances both from casual to formal attire.

Instructions are on p. 44.

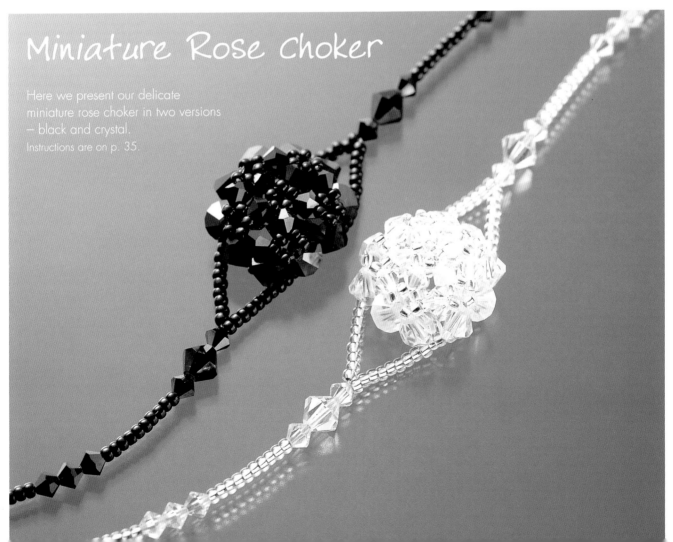

Miniature Rose Choker

Here we present our delicate miniature rose choker in two versions — black and crystal.

Instructions are on p. 35.

Antique Gold Ring & Necklace

The gold beads in these matching pieces exude a
lovely, mellow warmth.

Instructions are on pp. 46-48.

Eyeglass Chains

Eyeglass chains this beautiful are sure to appeal to women of all ages.
Attach your sunglasses to one of them, and wear it like a necklace.

Instructions are on p. 49.

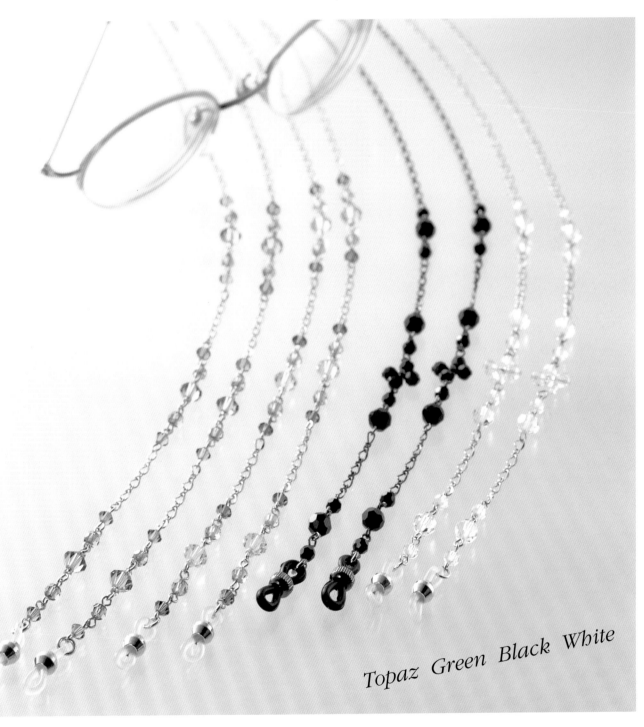

Topaz Green Black White

On this page you'll find photographs and brief descriptions of all the tools and supplies needed to make the jewelry in this book. Our instructions pages list all the items used to make each project.

● Faceted crystal beads (these are the stars of the Swarovski product line)

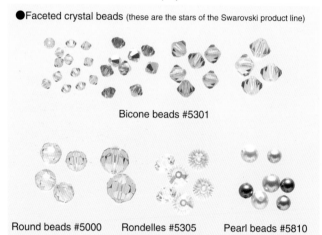

Bicone beads #5301

Round beads #5000   Rondelles #5305   Pearl beads #5810

Swarovski is renowned for high-quality crystal beads and lustrous pearl beads, which come in a broad spectrum of gorgeous colors.

● Czech faceted glass beads (fire-polished beads)

These are available in a wide range of colors, shapes and sizes.

● The key here is to select the appropriate size for the piece you are making. Elastic cord is most suitable for bracelets.

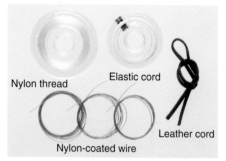

Nylon thread   Elastic cord

Nylon-coated wire   Leather cord

● All of these pliers are useful, but can substitute regular pliers for flat-nose pliers.

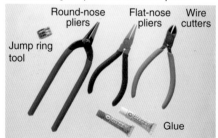

Jump ring tool

Round-nose pliers   Flat-nose pliers   Wire cutters

Glue

● Plastic pearl beads

These beads come in a bewildering array of colors. You might want to store each color separately, with identifying tags.

● Venetian glass beads

These beads can be expensive, but they will lend originality to your jewelry.

● Beads commonly used to make jewelry

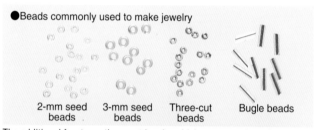

2-mm seed beads   3-mm seed beads   Three-cut beads   Bugle beads

The additional facets on three-cut beads, which are approximately the same size as the familiar 2-mm seed beads, add sparkle. Bugle beads come in many sizes, but we used 6-mm beads for the jewelry in this book.

● You'll need findings for practically every piece you make. Make sure you have the right size.

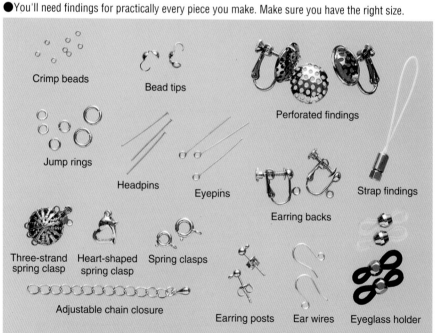

Crimp beads   Bead tips   Perforated findings

Jump rings

Headpins   Eyepins   Strap findings

Earring backs

Three-strand spring clasp   Heart-shaped spring clasp   Spring clasps

Adjustable chain closure

Earring posts   Ear wires   Eyeglass holder

BASIC TECHNIQUES

Here we present instructions for some basic techniques you will need to master to create truly beautiful jewelry. They are not difficult to learn. With a little practice, you'll be an expert before you know it!

● Opening and closing jump rings with a jump ring tool

1. Place the tool on your left thumb (or right thumb if you're left-handed). Grasp a jump ring with flat-nose pliers and insert it into the groove in the tool.

2. Open the jump ring by twisting it gently, upward, with the points of the pliers. Avoid pulling it sideways.

3. The jump ring is open when it looks like the one in the photo. Reverse this process to close it. There shouldn't be any space between the ends.

● Rounding the ends of eyepins or headpins.

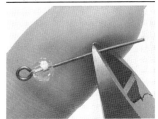

1. Insert the pin into one or more beads. Cut shaft of pin, leaving a 7-mm end.

● Working with crimp beads at the end of a necklace (or other piece of jewelry)

 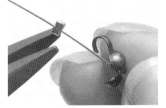 

1. Insert wire (or nylon thread) into a bead tip, then a crimp bead.

2. Compress the crimp bead by squeezing it vertically with flat-nose pliers (or regular pliers).

3. Cut wire (or nylon thread) with wire-cutters, leaving a 1-mm end.

2. Bend the end so that it is perpendicular to the part of the shaft holding the bead.

4. Insert crimp bead into bead tip; close bead tip with pliers.

5. Attach clasp (top) and adjustable chain closure (bottom) with jump rings.

6. Clasp and adjustable chain closures attached to bead tips.

3. Grasp the end of the pin with round-nose pliers, and round into a tiny circle.

● Rounding ends of headpins (or eyepins)

1. With flat-nose pliers, gently open the rounded end of the pin.

2. Attach desired component.

3. Reverse Step 1 to reclose the circle. Don't leave any space between ends.

4. Don't let go of the pin until you've finished forming the circle. Rotate your wrist, using the roundness of the plier points to form the circle.

Satin Ring & Necklace

Satin crystal beads in eight beautiful colors are used to make
this dazzling necklace and ring.
Instructions are on pp. 20-21.

Duet Ring & Slave Ring

Make several of these sparkling rings, so you'll have one for
every occasion and every mood.

Instructions are on pp. 20-21.

Black Pink Gold Aurora Blue

DUET RING (Shown on p. 19) Size: US 6 (Circumference: 51mm)

See p. 48 for color chart.

24 4-mm Swarovski bicone crystal beads	Satin (3 beads of each color)		Gold
	Siam satin	Aquamarine satin	12 light Colorado topaz satin
	Peridot satin	Rose satin	12 Dorado 2x
	Amethyst satin	Light Colorado topaz satin	
	Montana satin	Light amethyst satin	
106 2-mm seed beads or 3-cut beads 70cm #3 nylon thread	Toho CR539 (3-cut beads)		Toho 221 (bronze metallic seed beads)

◆Round 1

1. String a seed bead (starting bead) on center of nylon thread. Designate one end of the thread as A, and the other as B. Mark one end with an oil-based marking pen so you can easily distinguish it from the other.

2. String a bicone bead, a seed bead and a bicone bead on each half (A and B) of the nylon thread. (Refer to chart on p. 48 if you're using two colors of crystal beads.) Cross A and B over one another with a seed bead at the intersection; repeat twice (for a total of 3 times).

3. String 3 seed beads on each half of nylon thread (A and B), then cross A and B over one another with a seed bead at the intersection. Repeat this pattern 5 times (for a total of 6 times). If you need to make the ring larger or smaller, add or subtract a repetition. If you follow the instructions given above (6 repetitions), you should end up with a Size 6 ring.
From now on, make a check mark in the box at left each time you complete a step.

4. ☐String three seed beads on A, then pass A through the starting seed bead.
☐String a seed bead on A, and another on B. Cross A and B over one another with a seed bead at the intersection.

◆Round 2

5. String a seed bead on B, and 5 seed beads on A. Cross A and B over one another with a seed bead at the intersection (Fig. 2).

6. ☐Pass A through a bicone bead, a seed bead (① in Fig. 3), and then a bicone bead.
☐Pass B through a bicone bead, a seed bead, and a bicone bead. Cross A and B over one another with a seed bead at the intersection. Repeat until you reach ③.

7. ☐Pass B through a seed bead (④ in Fig. 3), then another seed bead.
☐Pass A through 2 seed beads, then cross A and B over one another with a seed bead at the intersection.

◆Repeat Step 7 until you reach ⑧ in Fig. 3.

(Fig. 3)

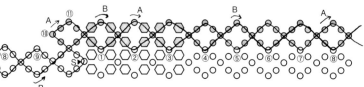

8. Pass A through a seed bead, through ⑨ in Fig. 4, through another seed bead, and through ⑩ (Fig. 4). Pass B through 3 seed beads. Tie A and B together twice, hide ends in adjacent beads, and cut excess thread.

(Fig. 1)

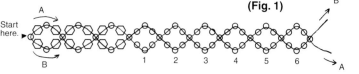

(Fig. 2)

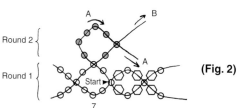

(Fig. 4)

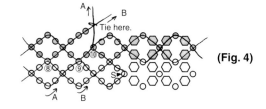

MULTICOLORED SATIN NECKLACE (shown on p. 18)   Finished length: 36cm

3-mm Swarovski bicone crystal beads	16 Montana satin	16 aquamarine satin	29 rose satin	29 Siam satin
4-mm Swarovski bicone crystal beads	13 Montana satin 29 amethyst satin	24 aquamarine satin 27 light Colorado satin	27 peridot satin	40 light amethyst satin
5-mm Swarovski bicone crystal beads	11 Montana satin 11 amethyst satin	13 peridot satin 13 light Colorado topaz satin	11 rose satin	11 Siam satin
3 50-cm lengths nylon-coated wire, 6 crimp beads, 6 jump rings, 6 bead tips, three-strand clasp set				

1. Attach a bead tip and crimp bead to one end of all 3 lengths of wire. Compress crimp bead, cut wire and close bead tip over crimp bead We will be referring to the 3 strands of wire as A, B and C.

2. String bicone beads on A, B and C, referring to Fig. 1 (on opposite page). You will be repeating 8 patterns. Follow the drawings with care, as the patterns are all different.

SLAVE RING (shown on pp. 18-19)

Size: US 6 (Circumference: 51mm) See p. 48 for color chart.

	Multicolored	Pink	Green	Black	Aurora	Blue
36 4-mm Swarovski bicone crystal beads	4 Siam satin 4 peridot satin 4 aquamarine satin 4 light Colorado topaz satin 5 rose satin 5 Montana satin 5 amethyst satin 5 light amethyst satin	18 fuchsia 18 amethyst satin 18 rose satin	18 light Colorado satin 18 peridot satin 18 lime	18 jet hematite 18 black diam ond 18 crystal	18 crystal AB 18 white opal	18 aquamarine satin 18 Montana satin 18 Capri blue satin
164 2-mm seed or 3-cut beads	Toho CR539 (rainbow 3-cut beads)	Toho CR356 (magenta-lined crystal luster 3-cut beads)	Toho 221 (bronze metallic seed beads)	Toho 49 (jet black seed beads)	Toho 1 (crystal transparent seed beads)	Toho CR540 (blue 3-cut beads)
80cm #3 nylon thread						

◆Follow instructions for the Duet Ring through Step 7.
1. In Step 8, pass A through ⑩, then a seed bead. Pass B through a seed bead, then cross A and B over one another with a seed bead at the intersection. Both lengths of nylon thread should now be at the top of your work.

◆Row 3 (Fig. 5)

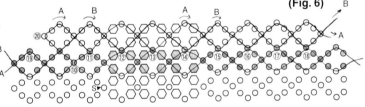

(Fig. 5)

Make a check mark in the box at left each time you complete a step.

2. ☐String a seed bead on B and 5 seed beads on A. Cross A and B over one another with a seed bead at the intersection.

3. ☐Pass A through a seed bead, through ⑪, then through another seed bead.
☐Pass B through 3 seed beads. Cross A and B over one another at the intersection.

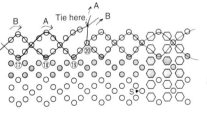

4. ☐Pass B through a bicone bead, through ⑫, and through another bicone bead.
Pass A through a bicone bead, a seed bead, and another bicone bead. Cross A and B over one another with a seed bead at the intersection.
☐Pass A through a bicone bead, ⑬, and another bicone bead.
Pass B through a bicone bead, a seed bead, and another bicone bead. Cross A and B over one another with a seed bead at the intersection.
☐Pass B through a bicone bead, ⑭, and another bicone bead.
Pass A through a bicone bead, a seed bead, and another bicone bead. Cross A and B over one another with a seed bead at the intersection.

5. ☐Pass A through a seed bead, ⑮, then another seed bead. Pass B through 2 seed beads. Cross A and B over one another with a seed bead at the intersection.
☐Pass B through a seed bead, ⑯, then another seed bead. Pass A through 2 seed beads. Cross A and B over one another with a seed bead at the intersection.

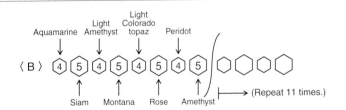

(Fig. 6)

6. Repeat Step 5 until you reach ⑱ (see Fig. 6).

7. ☐Pass A through a seed bead, ⑲, another seed bead, and then ⑳.
☐Pass B through 3 seed beads (Fig. 7).
Tie A and B together twice, hide ends in beads, and cut excess thread.

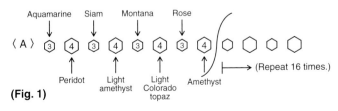

(Fig. 7)

3. When you've strung all the bicone beads, gather A, B and C together and twist into a spiral. (Add or subtract a bicone bead or two, if necessary, so that the beads on all three lengths of wire line up perfectly.) Attach bead tips, then crimp beads to A, B and C. Compress crimp beads, cut wire, and close bead tips over crimp beads.

4. Attach a three-strand clasp to ends with jump rings.

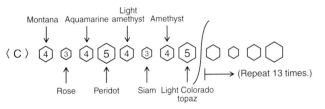

〈A〉 Aquamarine, Siam, Montana, Rose ... Peridot, Light amethyst, Light Colorado topaz, Amethyst → (Repeat 16 times.)

(Fig. 1)

〈B〉 Aquamarine, Light Amethyst, Light Colorado topaz, Peridot ... Siam, Montana, Rose, Amethyst → (Repeat 11 times.)

〈C〉 Montana, Aquamarine, Light amethyst, Amethyst ... Rose, Peridot, Siam, Light Colorado topaz → (Repeat 13 times.)

Ball Ring,
Necklace & Earrings

You'll get lots of compliments when you wear these graceful pieces.
Instructions are on pp. 24-25.

Blue Yellow Pink Purple

Black Red

Green Blue purple Crystal

Necklace with Tiny Balls

The tiny balls on this necklace sparkle like stars in a galaxy.
Instructions: p. 36

Black Pink

BALL RING (shown on p. 22)

Size: US 6 (Circumference: 51mm)

	Black	Red
12 4-mm Swarovski bicone crystal beads	Jet	Siam
80 2-mm seed beads	Toho 49 (jet black)	Toho 332 (raspberry gold luster)
Crimp bead, 30cm each #2 and #3 nylon thread		

Balls of this type are one of the basic forms used in bead jewelry. Remember that the last steps (beginning with the tying off of the thread ends) are the most crucial, and therefore the most important ones to master.

◆Make the ball.

1. Start out by stringing a bicone bead on the center of #2 nylon thread. Designate one side of the thread as A, and the other as B.

2. Pass each of A and B through its own bicone bead. Cross A and B over one another with a bicone bead at the intersection. Repeat this pattern twice, for a total of 3 repetitions (Fig. 1).

3. Pass each of A and B through a bicone bead. Cross A and B over one another with the first bicone bead strung at the intersection. Create a ball shape by pulling thread ends tightly (Fig. 2).

Make a check mark in the box at left each time you complete a step.

☐ When you hide the thread ends, pass A through ①②③④, and B through ⑤⑥⑦⑧). Then pass one end through the starting bead. Ends should now be next to each other.

☐ Tie A and B together twice tightly. Pass ends through adjacent beads and cut excess thread.

◆Make the band.

4. Pass the #3 nylon thread through the center of the ball. Designate one end of the thread as A, and the other as B. String 20 seed beads, a crimp bead, then 20 more seed beads on A. Pass A through the other side of the ball, forming a circle (Fig. 3).

5. String 20 seed beads on A and B. Cross A and B over one another with the crimp bead you added in Step 4 at the intersection. Compress the crimp bead with pliers; cut excess thread (Fig. 4). Adjust band length now, if necessary, by adding (or subtracting) seed beads. If you use 20 each time, you should end up with a US Size 6 ring.

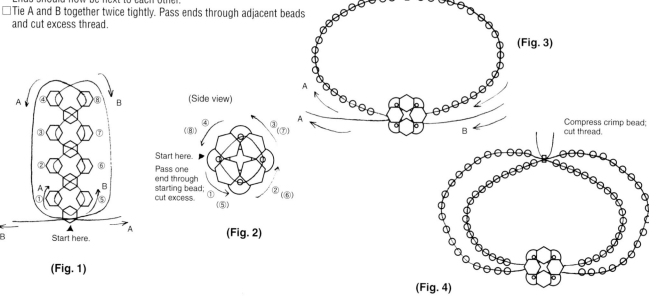

(Fig. 1)

(Fig. 2)

Start here.

(Side view)

Start here.
Pass one end through starting bead; cut excess.

(Fig. 3)

(Fig. 4)

Compress crimp bead; cut thread.

BALL EARRINGS (shown on p. 22)

	Blue	Yellow	Pink	Purple
24 4-mm Swarovski bicone crystal beads	Light sapphire	Jonquil	Light rose	Light amethyst
2 30-cm lengths nylon thread, 2 headpins, ear wires				

1. Make 2 balls, following Steps 1-3 of instructions for the ball ring.

◆Attach ear wires or earring backs.

2. Insert a headpin into the center of a 3-bicone-bead cluster (see drawing at right). Cut pin, leaving a 7 or 8-mm end. Round end with round-nose pliers (see p. 17).

3. Attach ear wire (or earring back) to rounded end of headpin. Repeat Steps 2 and 3 for other earring.

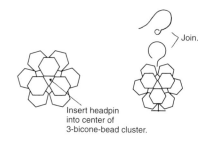

Join.

Insert headpin into center of 3-bicone-bead cluster.

BALL NECKLACE (shown on p. 22)

Finished length: 36cm

	Black	Red
32 4-mm Swarovski bicone crystal beads	Jet	Siam
8-mm Swarovski round crystal bead	Jet	Siam
200 2-mm seed beads	Toho 49 (jet black)	Toho 332 (raspberry gold luster)
30cm #2 nylon thread, 45cm nylon-coated wire, headpin, eyepin, 2 crimp beads, 2 bead tips, 2 jump rings, spring clasp, adjustable chain closure		

1. Make a bead ball with 4-mm bicone beads, following Steps 1-2 of instructions for ball ring.

◆Make center of necklace.

2. Insert an eyepin into center of a 3-bicone-bead cluster (Fig. 1). Cut pin, leaving a 7 or 8-mm end. Round end with round-nose pliers (see p. 17).

3. Insert a headpin into the 6-mm bicone bead. Cut pin, leaving a 7 or 8-mm end. Round end with round-nose pliers, and attach to eyepin from Step 2 (Fig. 2).

◆Make necklace.

4. String a bead tip on one end of wire, then a crimp bead. Compress crimp bead; cut wire, leaving a 1-mm end. Close bead tip over crimp bead.

Make a check mark in the boxes at left as you complete each step.

5. ☐String 6cm seed beads (about 45) on wire.
   ☐Add beads in the following order: 4-mm bicone bead, seed bead, 4-mm crystal bead, 10 seed beads. Repeat this pattern 4 times (for a total of 5 times).

6. ☐Pass wire through center of necklace.
   ☐Add beads in the following order: 10 seed beads, a 4-mm bicone bead, a seed bead, and a 4-mm bicone bead. Repeat this pattern 4 times (for a total of 5 times).
   ☐String 6cm seed beads (about 45) on wire (Fig. 3). (Bead sizes vary slightly, possibly even enough to make a difference, so make sure the two sides match as you go along.)

7. String a bead tip on end of wire, then a crimp bead. Compress crimp bead; cut wire. Close bead tip over crimp bead. Attach clasp and adjustable chain closure with jump rings.

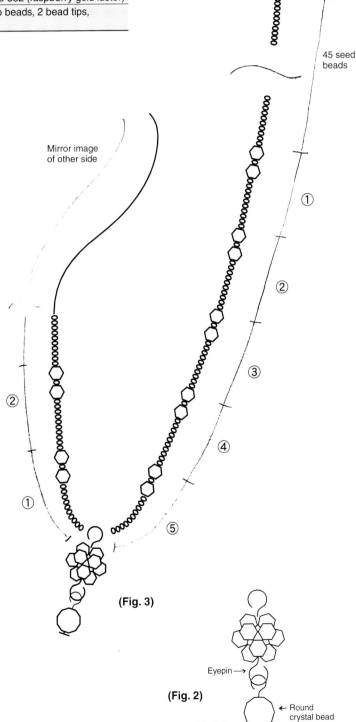

45 seed beads

Mirror image of other side

① ② ③ ④ ⑤

(Fig. 3)

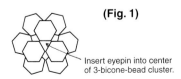

(Fig. 1)

Insert eyepin into center of 3-bicone-bead cluster.

(Fig. 2)

Eyepin →

Headpin →

← Round crystal bead

Multicolored Crystal Dome Ring, Necklace & Earrings

You'll be the envy of all your friends when you wear the multicolored set.
For a subtler but equally dramatic effect, try the monochrome pieces.
Instructions are on pp. 28-29 and p. 34.

Ruby Topaz

Colorful

CRYSTAL DOME RING (shown on p. 26)

Size: US 6 (Circumference: 51mm)

	Multicolored			Topaz	Ruby
37 4-mm Swarovski bicone beads	a. 2 Siam b. 3 Capri blue c. 2 fuchsia d. 2 lime e. 1 light amethyst	f. 1 amethyst g. 1 smoked topaz h. 2 black diamond i. 1 Montana j. 13 light Colorado topaz	k. 2 topaz l. 2 tourmaline m. 2 rose n. 2 olivine	Topaz	Ruby
103 2-mm seed beads 80cm #3 nylon thread	Toho 221 (bronze metallic)			Toho 221 (bronze metallic)	Toho 221 (bronze metallic)

These instructions are for the multicolored version of the ring. Match the lower-case letters with those in the chart above.

◆Make dome.

1. String a bicone bead (m) (starting bead) on center of nylon thread. Designate one end as A, and the other as B.
   Mark one end with an oil-based marking pen so you can easily distinguish it from the other.

   Make a check mark in the boxes at left as you complete each step.
   ☐String a seed bead on A.
   String a seed bead, a bicone bead ①, (h), then a seed bead on B.
   Cross A and B over one another with a bicone bead (l) at the intersection (Fig. 1).

2. ☐String a seed bead on B.
   Pass A through a seed bead, a bicone bead ② (c), then a seed bead.
   Cross A and B over one another with a bicone bead (e) at the intersection.
   ☐String a seed bead on A.
   Pass B through a seed bead, a bicone bead ③ (j), then a seed bead.
   Cross A and B over one another with a bicone bead (h) at the intersection.
   ☐String a seed bead on B.
   Pass A through a seed bead, a bicone bead ④ (d), then a seed bead.
   Cross A and B over one another with a bicone bead (b) at the intersection.
   ☐String a seed bead on A.
   Pass A through starting bead, then a seed bead.
   String a seed bead on B. Cross A and B over one another with a bicone bead (h) at the intersection (Fig. 2). You have now completed the central flower.

◆Now the dome will begin to look more three-dimensional.

3. ☐Pass A through a seed bead, a bicone bead ⑤ (i), then a seed bead.
   String a seed bead on B. Cross A and B over one another with a bicone bead (a) at the intersection.
   ☐Pass B through a seed bead, a bicone bead ⑥ (h), then a seed bead.
   String a seed bead on A. Cross A and B over one another with a bicone bead (e) at the intersection.
   ☐String a seed bead on B. Pass B through a bicone bead ①, then add another seed bead.
   String a seed bead on A. Cross A and B over one another with a bicone bead (g) at the intersection.
   ☐Pass B through a seed bead, a bicone bead ⑦ (k), then a seed bead.
   String a seed bead on A. Cross A and B over one another with a bicone bead (a) at the intersection.
   ☐Pass B through a seed bead, a bicone bead ②, then add another seed bead.
   String a seed bead on A. Cross A and B over one another with a bicone bead (d) at the intersection.
   ☐Pass B through a seed bead, a bicone bead ⑧ (b), then a seed bead.
   String a seed bead on A. Cross A and B over one another with a bicone bead (g) at the intersection.
   ☐Pass B through a seed bead, a bicone bead ③, then another seed bead.
   String a seed bead on A. Cross A and B over one another with a bicone bead (k) at the intersection.
   ☐Pass B through a seed bead, a bicone bead ⑨ (n), then a seed bead.
   String a seed bead on A. Cross A and B over one another with a bicone bead (f) at the intersection.

S = Starting bead

(Fig. 1)

(Fig. 2)

(Fig. 3)

Work around perimeter.

☐Pass B through a seed bead, a bicone bead ④, then a seed bead.
String a seed bead on A. Cross A and B over one another with a bicone bead (a) at the intersection.
☐String a seed bead, a bicone bead ⑤, then a seed bead on A.
String a seed bead on B. Cross A and B over one another with a bicone bead (l) at the intersection.
The piece should resemble a dome now (Fig. 3).

◆Work around the perimeter of the dome, inserting two seed beads between bicone beads (Fig. 3).

4. ☐String 2 seed beads on B. Pass B through a bicone bead ⑥ (h), then 2 seed beads.
   Pass B through a bicone bead ⑦ (k), then 2 seed beads.
   Pass B through a bicone bead ⑧ (b), then 2 seed beads.
   Pass B through a bicone bead ⑨, then Cross A and B over one another with 2 seed beads at the intersection.
   The dome is now completed.

◆Weave the band, continuing with the same thread.

Rear view of dome

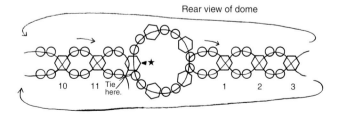

Tie here.

5. String 2 seed beads on A and 2 on B. Cross A and B over one another with a bicone bead (j) at the intersection. Repeat this pattern 11 times. Work the pattern a 12th time without forming an intersection. Tie A and B together tightly. Hide thread ends in adjacent beads and cut excess.

CRYSTAL DOME NECKLACE (shown on p. 26)

Finished length: 36cm

	Multicolored			Topaz	Ruby
100 4-mm Swarovski bicone beads	a. 7 Siam b. 8 Capri blue c. 8 fuchsia d. 7 lime e. 6 light amethyst	f. 6 amethyst g. 8 smoked topaz h. 7 black diamond i. 8 Montana j. 8 light Colorado topaz	k. 8 topaz l. 6 tourmaline m. 6 rose n. 7 olivine	Topaz	Ruby
130 2-mm seed beads	Toho 221 (bronze metallic)			Toho 221 (bronze metallic)	Toho 221 (bronze metallic)
70cm #3 nylon thread, 45-cm nylon-coated wire, 2 crimp beads, 2 bead tips, 2 jump rings, spring clasp, adjustable chain closure					

These instructions are for the multicolored version of the necklace.
Match the lower-case letters with those in the chart above.
◆Make dome, referring to Steps 1-3 on p. 28.

Make a check mark in the boxes at left as you complete each step.
4. ☐String a seed bead, a bicone bead ⑩ (m), then a seed bead on A.
  String a seed bead on B. Cross A and B over one another with a bicone bead (d) at the intersection.
  ☐Pass A through a seed bead, a bicone bead ⑥, then another seed bead.
  String a seed bead on B. Cross A and B over one another with a bicone bead (f) at the intersection.
  ☐Pass B through a seed bead, a bicone bead ⑦, then a seed bead.
  Pass A through a seed bead. Cross A and B over one another with a bicone bead (c) at the intersection.
  ☐Pass A through a seed bead, a bicone bead ⑧, then a seed bead.
  Pass B through a seed bead. Cross A and B over one another with a bicone bead (i) at the intersection.
  ☐Pass B through a seed bead, a bicone bead ⑨, a seed bead, then a bicone bead ⑩. Cross A and B over one another with a seed bead at the intersection.
  You have formed a sphere (Fig. 4).

5. Pass A or B through 2-3 beads, bringing it out next to the other end.
  Tie ends tightly. Hide ends in adjacent beads; cut excess thread.

◆Make necklace (Fig. 5).
6. String a bead tip on one end of wire, then a crimp bead.
  Compress crimp bead; cut wire, leaving a 1-mm end.
  Close bead tip over crimp bead (see p. 17).

7. String 70 seed beads and bicone beads (35 each on each side), alternating between the two types of beads. (Make sure the two sides are identical.) Make adjustments for size here by adding or subtracting beads.

8. Pass wire through dome. String remaining seed and bicone beads. String a bead tip and a crimp bead on wire. Compress crimp bead, cut wire, and close bead tip over crimp bead. Attach a spring clasp to one end of necklace, and an adjustable chain closure to other end.

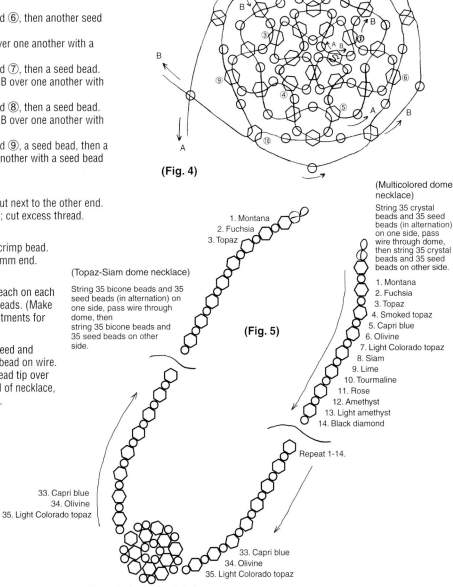

(Fig. 4)

1. Montana
2. Fuchsia
3. Topaz

(Topaz-Siam dome necklace)
String 35 bicone beads and 35 seed beads (in alternation) on one side, pass wire through dome, then string 35 bicone beads and 35 seed beads on other side.

(Fig. 5)

33. Capri blue
34. Olivine
35. Light Colorado topaz

33. Capri blue
34. Olivine
35. Light Colorado topaz

Pass wire through beads in dome.

(Multicolored dome necklace)
String 35 crystal beads and 35 seed beads (in alternation) on one side, pass wire through dome, then string 35 crystal beads and 35 seed beads on other side.

1. Montana
2. Fuchsia
3. Topaz
4. Smoked topaz
5. Capri blue
6. Olivine
7. Light Colorado topaz
8. Siam
9. Lime
10. Tourmaline
11. Rose
12. Amethyst
13. Light amethyst
14. Black diamond

Repeat 1-14.

Rose Ring & Necklace

Crystal beads add extra elegance to these pretty pieces.
Instructions are on pp. 32-33.

Purple Black Topaz Green Red Blue

Red Purple Green Black

Grape Cluster Earrings & Simple Necklace

The two-color combination of crystal beads reflects light beautifully.

Instructions are on pp. 35-36.

Black Green Red

ROSE RING (shown on p. 30)

Size: US 6 (Circumference: 51mm)

	Blue	Purple
32 4-mm Swarovski bicone crystal beads	27 aquamarine satin 5 Montana satin	27 amethyst satin 5 violet
10 6-mm Swarovski bicone crystal beads	Aquamarine satin	Amethyst satin
108 2-mm seed beads	Toho 82 (navy iris metallic)	Toho 205 (light amethyst gold luster)
2 lengths #3 nylon thread (25cm and 80cm)		

◆Make miniature rose.

Unless otherwise specified, use 4-mm bicone beads. String a bicone bead (a) on center of 80cm nylon thread (this is your starting bead). Designate one end of the thread as A, and the other as B. Mark one end with an oil-based marking pen so you can easily distinguish it from the other.

Make a check mark in the boxes at left as you complete each step.

1. ☐String a seed bead on A.
   Pass B through a seed bead, a bicone bead (b) ①, then a seed bead. Cross A and B over one another with a bicone bead (a) at the intersection (Fig. 1).

2. ☐String a seed bead on B.
   Pass A through a seed bead, a bicone bead (b) ②, then a seed bead. Cross A and B over one another with a bicone bead (a) at the intersection.
   ☐String a seed bead on A.
   Pass B through a seed bead, a bicone bead (b) ③, then a seed bead. Cross A and B over one another with a bicone bead (a) at the intersection.
   ☐String a seed bead on B.
   Pass A through a seed bead, a bicone bead (b) ④, then a seed bead. Cross A and B over one another with a bicone bead (a) at the intersection.
   ☐Pass A through a seed bead, starting bead, and another seed bead. Pass B through a seed bead. Cross A and B over one another with a bicone bead (b) at the intersection.
   You have completed the miniature rose.

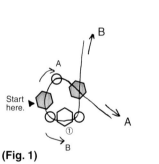

(Fig. 1)

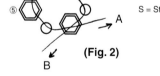

(Fig. 2)

S = Starting bead

◆Now make the outer periphery of the flower with 6-mm crystal beads (Fig. 2).

3. ☐Pass A through a seed bead, a 6-mm bicone bead ⑤, then a seed bead. Pass B through a seed bead. Cross A and B over one another with a 6-mm bicone bead at the intersection.
   ☐Pass B through a seed bead, a 6-mm bicone bead (b) ⑥, then a seed bead. Pass A through a seed bead. Cross A and B over one another with a 6-mm bicone bead at the intersection.
   ☐Pass B through a seed bead, a 6-mm bicone bead ①, then a seed bead. Pass A through a seed bead. Cross A and B over one another with a 6-mm bicone bead at the intersection.
   ☐Pass B through a seed bead, a 6-mm bicone bead ⑦ (a), then a seed bead. Pass A through a seed bead. Cross A and B over one another with a 6-mm bicone bead at the intersection.

☐Pass B through a seed bead, a 6-mm bicone bead ②, then a seed bead. Pass A through a seed bead. Cross A and B over one another with a 6-mm bicone bead at the intersection.
☐Pass B through a seed bead, a 6-mm bicone bead ⑧ (a), then a seed bead. Pass A through a seed bead. Cross A and B over one another with a 6-mm bicone bead at the intersection.
☐Pass B through a seed bead, a 6-mm bicone bead ③, then a seed bead. Pass A through a seed bead. Cross A and B over one another with a 6-mm bicone bead at the intersection.
☐Pass B through a seed bead, a 6-mm bicone bead ⑨, then a seed bead. Pass A through a seed bead. Cross A and B over one another with a 6-mm bicone bead at the intersection.
☐Pass A through a seed bead, a 6-mm bicone bead ④, then a seed bead. Pass B through a seed bead. Cross A and B over one another with a 6-mm bicone bead at the intersection.
☐Pass A through a seed bead, a 6-mm bicone bead ⑤, then a seed bead. Pass B through a seed bead. Cross A and B over one another with a 6-mm bicone bead (a) at the intersection.

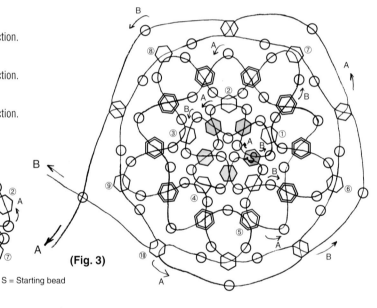

(Fig. 3)

◆Close back of rose (Fig. 3).

4. ☐Pass A through a seed bead, a bicone bead (a) ⑩, then a seed bead. Pass B through a seed bead. Cross A and B over one another with a bicone bead (a) at the intersection.
   ☐Pass A through a seed bead, a bicone bead ⑥, then a seed bead. Pass B through a seed bead. Cross A and B over one another with a bicone bead (a) at the intersection.
   ☐Pass B through a seed bead, a bicone bead ⑦, then a seed bead. Pass A through a seed bead. Cross A and B over one another with a bicone bead (a) at the intersection.
   ☐Pass A through String a seed bead, a bicone bead ⑧, then a seed bead. Pass B through a seed bead. Cross A and B over one another with a bicone bead (a) at the intersection.
   ☐Pass B through a seed bead, a bicone bead ⑨, a seed bead, then a bicone bead ⑩. Cross A and B over one another with a seed bead at the intersection.

5. Pass A or B through beads around perimeter of rose, bringing it out next to other end. Tie ends tightly. Hide in 2-3 adjacent beads; cut excess thread.

◆Make the band (Fig. 4)

6. At the back of the rose, pass 25cm nylon thread through the 2 beads indicated by the ☆ symbol.
Make sure left and right lengths of thread are the same length. (Both sides of the rose are identical, but it's better to cut the thread at the back.)

7. String 2 seed beads on each side of thread. Cross ends over one another with a 4-mm bicone bead at the intersection.
Repeat this pattern a total of 11 times. Work the pattern a 12th time without forming an intersection. Pass one end through beads, bringing it out at ★ symbol. Tie ends together tightly.
Hide in adjacent beads and cut excess.

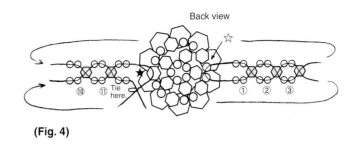

Back view

(Fig. 4)

MINIATURE ROSE NECKLACE (shown on p. 30)

Finished length: 42cm

	Amethyst	Jet	Topaz	Peridot	Rose
58 4-mm Swarovski bicone crystal beads	(a) 53 amethyst satin (b) 5 violet	(a) 53 jet hematite (b) 5 jet hematite	(a) 53 light Colorado topaz satin (b) 5 smoked topaz	(a) 53 peridot satin (b) 5 tourmaline	(a) 53 rose satin (b) 5 Siam satin
10 6-mm Swarovski bicone crystal beads	Amethyst satin	Jet hematite	Light Colorado topaz satin	Peridot satin	Rose satin
260 2-mm seed beads	Toho 205 (light amethyst gold luster)	Toho 49 (jet black)	Toho 221 (bronze metallic)	Toho 84 (green iris metallic)	Toho 332 (raspberry gold luster)
80cm #3 nylon thread, 50cm nylon-coated wire, 2 crimp beads, 2 bead tips, 2 jump rings, spring clasp, adjustable chain closure					

◆Make miniature rose, referring to Steps 1-5 of instructions for miniature rose ring on previous page.

◆Make necklace (Fig. 1).
1. String a bead tip on one end of wire, then a crimp bead. Compress crimp bead; cut wire, leaving a 1-mm end. Close bead tip over crimp bead (see p. 17).

2. String 5 seed beads and 1 4-mm bicone bead (a) on wire. Repeat 19 times, then add 5 more seed beads.

3. Pass wire through 2 seed beads indicated by ☆ symbol on back of miniature rose. Pick up nylon thread on inside and bring wire out on other side (Fig. 2).

4. String 5 seed beads and 1 bicone bead (a). Repeat 19 times, then add 5 more seed beads. Pass end of wire through a bead tip, then a crimp bead. Compress crimp bead; cut wire and close bead tip over crimp bead.

5. Attach a spring clasp to one end of necklace, and an adjustable chain closure to other end with jump rings.

(Back view)

(Fig. 2)

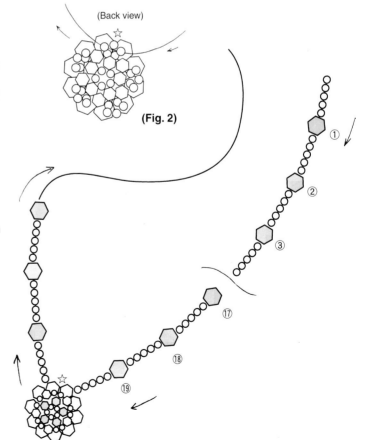

(Fig. 1)

MULTICOLORED CRYSTAL DOME EARRINGS (shown on p. 27)

30 3-mm Swarovski bicone crystal beads	4 Siam	4 lime	4 olivine	4 Capri blue			
	2 rose	2 topaz	2 Montana	2 amethyst	2 fuchsia	2 light amethyst	2 black diamond
60 2-mm seed beads	Toho 221 (bronze metallic)						
2 beads equivalent in size to the 3-mm bicone beads (use inexpensive beads, as these will not show), 2 50-cm lengths #2 nylon thread, 2 headpins, ear wires (or earring backs)							

◆Make the dome.

1. Plan your color scheme so that beads of the same color don't adjoin one another. String a bicone bead (m) on the center of 50cm nylon thread (this is your starting bead). Designate one end of the thread as A, and the other as B. Mark one end with an oil-based marking pen so you can easily distinguish it from the other.

Make a check mark in the boxes at left as you complete each step.

☐ String a seed bead on A.
Pass B through a seed bead, a bicone bead ①, then a seed bead. Cross A and B over one another with a bicone bead at the intersection (Fig. 1).

(Fig. 1)

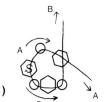

S = Starting bead

2. ☐ String a seed bead on B.
Pass A through a seed bead, a bicone bead ②, then a seed bead. Cross A and B over one another with a bicone bead at the intersection.
☐ String a seed bead on A.
Pass B through a seed bead, a bicone bead ③, then a seed bead. Cross A and B over one another with a bicone bead at the intersection.
☐ String a seed bead on B.
Pass B through a seed bead, a bicone bead ④, then a seed bead. Cross A and B over one another with a bicone bead at the intersection.
☐ Pass A through a seed bead, the starting bead, then another seed bead.
Pass B through a seed bead. Cross A and B over one another with a bicone bead at the intersection (Fig. 2). You have completed the central flower.

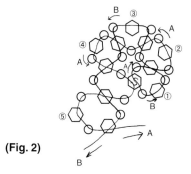

(Fig. 2)

3. ☐ Pass A through a seed bead, a bicone bead ⑤, then a seed bead.
Pass B through a seed bead. Cross A and B over one another with a bicone bead at the intersection.
☐ Pass A through a seed bead, a bicone bead ①, then a seed bead.
Pass B through a seed bead. Cross A and B over one another with a bicone bead at the intersection.

☐ Pass B through a seed bead, a bicone bead ②, then a seed bead.
Pass A through a seed bead. Cross A and B over one another with a bicone bead at the intersection.
☐ Pass A through a seed bead, a bicone bead ③, then a seed bead.
Pass B through a seed bead. Cross A and B over one another with a bicone bead at the intersection.
☐ Pass B through a seed bead, a bicone bead ④, then a seed bead.
Pass A through a seed bead, a bicone bead ⑤, then a seed bead (Fig. 3).

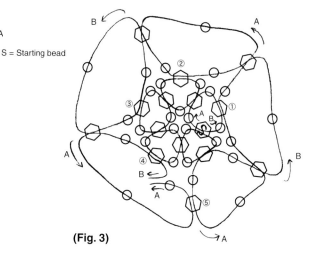

(Fig. 3)

●Before you tie threads to close dome, insert components that will attach to ear wires (Fig. 4).

4. ☐ Insert headpin into a bead equivalent in size to a 3-mm bicone bead. Round end of headpin. Leave a longer end than usual (about 1cm).
☐ Insert the bead into the dome so that the rounded end of the headpin protrudes to the outside. Tie threads together twice to close dome.
☐ Pass thread through 2-3 adjacent beads; cut excess (see Fig. 4 on p. 20).

5. Attach ear wires (or earring backs) to headpins (Fig. 5).

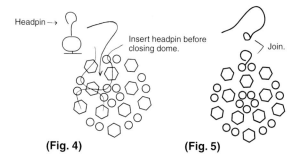

Headpin →

Insert headpin before closing dome.

Join.

(Fig. 4)　　　　**(Fig. 5)**

ROSE CHOKER (shown on p. 13)

Finished length: 31cm

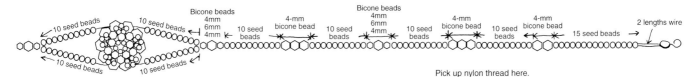

	Jet	Crystal
44 4-mm Swarovski bicone crystal beads	Jet hematite	Crystal AB
14 6-mm Swarovski bicone crystal beads	Jet hematite	Crystal AB
210 2-mm seed beads	Toho 49 (jet black)	Toho 21 (silver-lined crystal)
80 cm #3 nylon thread, 2 40-cm lengths nylon-coated wire, 2 crimp beads, 2 bead tips, 2 jump rings, spring clasp, adjustable chain closure		

◆Make miniature rose, following Steps 1-5 of instructions for miniature rose ring on p. 32.

Make a check mark in the boxes at left as you complete each step.
1. ☐Pass both lengths of wire through a bead tip, then a crimp bead. Compress crimp bead; cut wire, leaving a 1-mm end, and close bead tip over crimp bead (see p. 17).

◆String beads on the joined lengths of wire, as follows.
2. ☐15 seed beads and 2 4-mm bicone beads
   ☐10 seed beads and 3 4-mm bicone beads
   ☐10 seed beads, 1 4-mm bicone bead, 1 6-mm bicone bead, 1 4-mm bicone bead
   ☐10 seed beads, 3 4-mm bicone beads
   ☐10 seed beads, 1 4-mm bicone bead, 1 6-mm bicone bead, 1 4-mm bicone bead

3. Divide wire and string 10 seed beads, the miniature rose, and 10 more seed beads on each side.

◆From here on you'll be stringing beads on both lengths of wire at the same time, as before.
4. ☐1 4-mm bicone bead, 1 6-mm bicone bead, 1 4-mm bicone bead, 10 seed beads
   ☐3 4-mm bicone beads, 10 seed beads
   ☐1 4-mm bicone bead, 1 6-mm bicone bead, 1 4-mm bicone bead, 10 seed beads
   ☐3 4-mm bicone beads, 10 seed beads
   ☐2 4-mm bicone beads, 15 seed beads.

5. Pass both lengths of wire through a bead tip, then a crimp bead. Compress crimp bead and close bead tip over crimp bead. Attach a spring clasp and adjustable chain closure with jump rings.

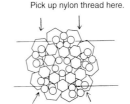

10 seed beads · 10 seed beads · Bicone beads 4mm 6mm 4mm · 10 seed beads · 4-mm bicone bead · 10 seed beads · Bicone beads 4mm 6mm 4mm · 10 seed beads · 4-mm bicone bead · 10 seed beads · 4-mm bicone bead · 15 seed beads · 2 lengths wire

10 seed beads · 10 seed beads

←— Work in mirror image of opposite side.

Pick up nylon thread here.

GRAPE CLUSTER EARRINGS (shown on p. 31)

	Red	Purple	Green	Black
32 4-mm Swarovski bicone crystal beads	16 Siam satin	16 amethyst satin	16 peridot satin	16 jet hematite
	16 rose satin	16 light amethyst	16 green tourmaline	16 crystal CAL
32 headpins, 8 0.8 x 4-mm jump rings, 2 0.8 x 4.5-mm jump rings, ear wires (or earring backs)				

1. Insert a headpin into each of the bicone beads; round ends (see p. 17).

2. To the 4 jump rings attach 1, 3, 5, or 7 headpins (attached to bicone beads in Step 1). (Aim for a nice balance between the two colors.)

3. Join jump rings. Make sure that the headpins don't end up clumped together in one place. Divide them between right and left as much as possible.

4. Attach ear wires (or earring backs) to the jump rings with 7 headpins on them.

5. Make other earring.

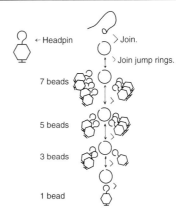

←Headpin · ⟩Join. · ⟩Join jump rings. · 7 beads · 5 beads · 3 beads · 1 bead

NECKLACE WITH TINY BALLS (shown on p. 23)

Finished length: 42cm

	Black	Pink	Green	Blue	Purple	Crystal
120 3-mm Swarovski bicone crystal beads	Jet hematite	Rose satin	Peridot	Light sapphire	Light amethyst	Crystal AB
11 4-mm Swarovski bicone crystal beads	Jet hematite	Rose satin	Peridot	Light sapphire	Light amethyst	Crystal AB
44 3-mm pearl beads	Metallic gray	Metallic rose	Pastel green	Pastel blue	Pastel purple	Off-white
2 50-cm lengths #6 nylon thread, 2 crimp beads, 2 bead tips, 2 jump rings, spring clasp, adjustable chain closure						

1. Make 10 bead balls using 3-mm bicone beads, referring to Steps 1-3 of instructions for ball ring on p. 24.

2. Pass the 2 lengths of #6 nylon thread through a bead tip, then a crimp bead. Compress crimp bead and close bead tip over crimp bead (see p. 17).

◆ Now you'll be stringing pearl beads and bead balls on the nylon thread. After all the beads have been strung, move them along the thread until they look the way you want them to.

Make a check mark in the boxes at left as you complete each step.
3. ☐ String a pearl bead on each length of thread.
   ☐ String a 4-mm bicone bead on both lengths of thread.
   ☐ String a pearl bead on each length of thread.
   ☐ Pass both lengths of thread through center of a bead ball, where 4 crystal beads converge.

4. Repeat pattern in Step 3 nine times (for a total of 10 patterns).

5. ☐ String a pearl bead on each strand of thread.
   ☐ String a 4-mm bicone bead on both strands of thread.
   ☐ String a pearl bead on each strand of thread.

6. Pass both lengths of thread through a bead tip, then a crimp bead. Compress crimp bead and close bead tip over crimp bead. Attach a spring clasp to one end and an adjustable chain closure to the other with jump rings.

7. Rearrange beads and bead balls attractively.

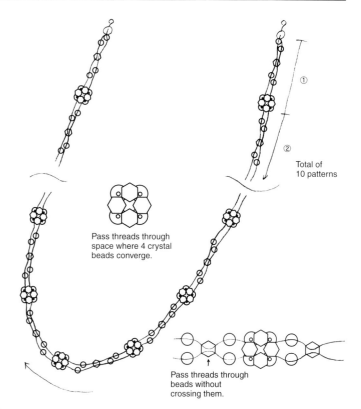

Total of 10 patterns

Pass threads through space where 4 crystal beads converge.

Pass threads through beads without crossing them.

SIMPLE NECKLACE (shown on p. 31)

Finished length: 36cm

	Black	Green	Red
76 4-mm Swarovski bicone crystal beads	Jet hematite	Peridot satin	Siam satin
57 2-mm seed beads	Toho 81 (hematite metallic)	Toho 3-cut 119 (olivine transparent luster)	Toho 332 (raspberry gold luster)
20 3-mm seed beads	Toho 81	Miyuki H3776 (green)	Toho 332
45cm nylon-coated wire, 10 headpins, 2 crimp beads, 2 bead tips, 2 jump rings, spring clasp, adjustable chain closure			

1. Insert headpins into l0 crystal beads; round ends (see p. 17).

2. Pass end of wire through a bead tip, then a crimp bead. Compress crimp bead; cut wire and close bead tip over crimp bead.

3. String a 2-mm seed bead, then a bicone bead on wire. Repeat this pattern 23 more times.

4. String a 3-mm seed bead, a prepared headpin, then a 3-mm seed bead on wire.

5. Referring to drawing, string a bicone bead, a 2-mm seed bead, a bicone bead, then a 3-mm seed bead. Repeat this pattern 8 more times.

6. Working in mirror image with Step 3, string a bicone bead, then a 2-mm seed bead on wire. Repeat this pattern 23 more times.

7. Pass end of wire through a bead tip, then a crimp bead. Compress crimp bead and close bead tip over crimp bead. Attach spring clasp to one end of necklace, and an adjustable chain closure to other end with jump rings.

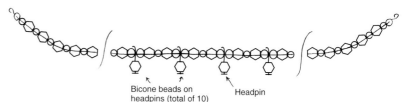

Bicone beads on headpins (total of 10)

Headpin

PEARL BRACELET (shown on p. 4)

Finished length: 26cm

	Gold	Silver	Crystal
86 4-mm Swarovski pearl beads	Gold	Light gray	Cream rose
19 5-mm Swarovski pearl beads	Gold	Light gray	Cream rose
81 4-mm Swarovski bicone crystal beads	Aurum	23 crystal CAL	Crystal AB
		58 crystal satin	
39 5-mm Swarovski bicone crystal beads	Dorado	Crystal CAL	Crystal AB
5 20-cm lengths strong elastic cord			

1. Referring to drawings, string beads on 5 separate lengths strong elastic cord.
   A: String 4-mm and 5-mm pearl beads in alternation.
   B: String 5-mm bicone beads.
   C: String 4-mm pearl beads.
   D: String 4-mm pearl beads and 4-mm bicone beads in alternation (for the silver bracelet, use crystal CAL).
   E: String 4-mm bicone beads (for the silver bracelet, use crystal satin beads).

2. Tie elastic cord at both ends of each strand tightly, twice.

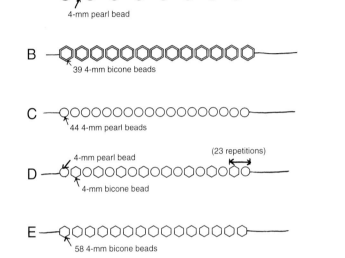

It isn't easy to thread elastic cord through pearl beads. Your work will go much faster if you use a threader like the one shown below, which is made of very fine wire.

SIMPLE ANKLET

Finished length: 20cm

48 4-mm Swarovski bicone crystal beads	Crystal
3-mm seed beads	Toho 21 (silver-lined crystal)
2-mm seed beads	Toho 21 (silver-lined crystal)
30cm #6 nylon thread, 2 crimp beads, 2 bead tips, 3 jump rings, spring clasp, adjustable chain closure, 16 headpins	

1. Insert a headpin into a bicone bead; round end (see p. 17). Make 16 of these components. Attach one of them to the end of an adjustable chain closure (cut to 2cm) with a jump ring.

2. Pass one end of wire through a bead tip, then a crimp bead. Compress crimp bead and close bead tip over crimp bead (see p. 17).

3. String a bicone bead, a 2-mm seed bead, a bicone bead, a 3-mm seed bead, and a prepared headpin (made in Step 1) on wire. Repeat this pattern 14 more times. End with a bicone bead, a 2-mm seed bead, and a bicone bead.

4. Pass wire through a bead tip, then a crimp bead. Compress crimp bead and close bead tip over crimp bead. Attach one end to a spring clasp, and the other to the other end of adjustable chain closure with jump rings.

2-mm seed bead   3-mm seed bead

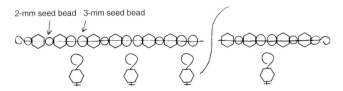

RING (shown on pp. 2-3, 5)

Size: US 6 (Circumference: 51mm)

	Black	Pink	Blue	Topaz	Aurora	Green
10 4-mm Swarovski bicone beads	(a) 5 crystal CAL (b) 5 jet	(a) 5 rose satin (b) 5 Siam satin	(a) 5 aquamarine satin (b) 5 Montana satin	(a) 5 light peach (b) 5 light Colorado topaz satin	(a) 5 crystal AB (b) 5 crystal AB	(a) 5 tourmaline (b) 5 peridot satin
10 5-mm Swarovski bicone beads	Jet	Siam satin	Montana satin	Light Colorado topaz satin	Crystal AB	Peridot satin
16 4-mm pearl beads 98 2-mm seed beads	Metallic gray Toho 81 (hematite metallic)	Metallic pink Toho 332 (raspberry gold luster)	Metallic silver Toho 82 (navy iris metallic)	Metallic beige Toho 221 (bronze metallic)	Off white Toho 21 (silver-lined crystal)	Metallic green Toho 84 (green iris metallic)
80cm #3 nylon thread						

◆Make dome.

String a bicone bead (a) (starting bead) on center of nylon thread. Designate one end as A, and the other as B. Mark one end with an oil-based marking pen so you can easily distinguish it from the other.

Make a check mark in the boxes at left as you complete each step.

1. ☐String a seed bead on A.
   Pass B through a seed bead, a pearl bead ①, then a seed bead. Cross A and B over one another with a bicone bead (a) at the intersection.

(Fig. 1) Start here.

2. ☐String a seed bead on B.
   Pass B through a seed bead, a pearl bead ②, then a seed bead. Cross A and B over one another with a bicone bead (a) at the intersection.
   ☐String a seed bead on A.
   Pass B through a seed bead, a pearl bead ③, then a seed bead. Cross A and B over one another with a bicone bead (a) at the intersection.
   ☐String a seed bead on B.
   Pass A through a seed bead, a pearl bead ④, then a seed bead. Cross A and B over one another with a bicone bead (a) at the intersection.
   ☐String a seed bead on A. Pass A through starting bead, then a seed bead.
   ☐String a seed bead on B. Cross A and B over one another with a pearl bead at the intersection. You have now completed the central flower (Fig. 2).

(Fig. 2)

S = Starting bead

◆Continue, referring to Fig. 3.

3. ☐Pass A through a seed bead, a 5-mm bicone bead ⑤, then a seed bead. String a seed bead on B. Cross A and B over one another with a 5-mm bicone bead at the intersection.
   ☐Pass B through a seed bead, a bicone bead (b), then a seed bead. Pass A through a seed bead. Cross A and B over one another with a 5-mm bicone bead at the intersection.
   ☐Pass B through a seed bead, a pearl bead ①, then a seed bead. String a seed bead on A. Cross A and B over one another with a 5-mm bicone bead at the intersection.
   ☐Pass B through a seed bead, a bicone bead (b), then a seed bead. String a seed bead on A. Cross A and B over one another with a 5-mm bicone bead at the intersection.
   ☐Pass B through a seed bead, a pearl bead ②, then a seed bead. String a seed bead on A. Cross A and B over one another with a 5-mm bicone bead at the intersection.
   ☐Pass B through a seed bead, a bicone bead (b), then a seed bead. String a seed bead on A. Cross A and B over one another with a 5-mm bicone bead at the intersection.
   ☐Pass B through a seed bead, a bicone bead ③, then another seed bead. String a seed bead on A. Cross A and B over one another with a 5-mm bicone bead at the intersection.
   ☐Pass B through a seed bead, a 5-mm bicone bead (b), then a seed bead. String a seed bead on A. Cross A and B over one another with a 5-mm bicone bead at the intersection.
   ☐Pass B through a seed bead, a pearl bead ④, then a seed bead. String a seed bead on A. Cross A and B over one another with a 5-mm bicone bead at the intersection.
   ☐Pass A through a seed bead, a 5-mm bicone bead ⑤, then a seed bead. String a seed bead on B. Cross A and B over one another with a bicone bead (b) at the intersection.

◆Work around the circumference of the dome, inserting two seed beads between bicone beads.

4. ☐String 2 seed beads on B. Pass B through a bicone bead (b) ⑥, then add 2 more seed beads.
   ☐Pass B through a bicone bead (b) ⑦ (k), then add 2 seed beads.
   ☐Pass B through a bicone bead (b) ⑧ (b), then add 2 seed beads.
   ☐Pass B through a bicone bead (b) ⑨, then cross A and B over one another with 2 seed beads at the intersection.
   The dome is now completed.

◆Continue weaving (the band, this time) with the same thread (Fig. 4).

5. String 2 seed beads on each of A and B. Cross A and B over one another with a bicone bead at the intersection. Repeat this pattern 11 times. Work the pattern a 12th time without forming an intersection. Pass thread through bead indicated by ★. in drawing. Tie A and B together tightly. Hide ends in adjacent beads and cut excess.

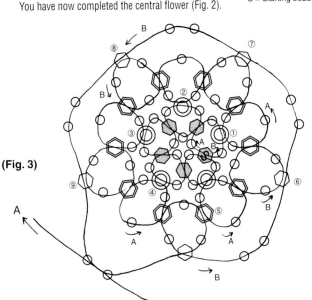

(Fig. 3)

Rear view

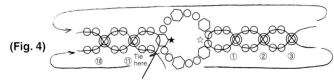

(Fig. 4) Tie here.

TWISTED NECKLACE FEATURING
PEARL AND CRYSTAL BEADS (Shown on pp. 2-3)

Finished length: c. 42cm

	Black	Pink	Blue	Topaz	Aurora	Green
46 4-mm Swarovski bicone crystal beads	Jet	Rose satin	Montana satin	Light Colorado topaz satin	Crystal AB	Peridot satin
45 5-mm Swarovski bicone crystal beads	Jet	Rose satin	Montana satin	Light Colorado topaz satin	Crystal AB	Peridot satin
72 pearl beads	Metallic black	Metallic pink	Metallic blue	Metallic beige	Off-white	Metallic green
73 2-mm seed beads	Toho 81 (hematite metallic)	Toho 332 (raspberry gold luster)	Toho 82 (navy iris metallic)	Toho 221 (bronze metallic)	Toho 21 (silver-lined crystal)	Toho 84 (green iris metallic)
2 50-cm lengths nylon-coated wire, 2 crimp beads, 2 bead tips, 2 jump rings, spring clasp, adjustable chain closure						

1. Pass both lengths of wire through a bead tip, then a crimp bead. Compress crimp bead; cut wire, leaving a 1-mm end, and close bead tip over crimp bead (see p. 17).

2. On one wire, string 4-mm and 5-mm bicone beads in alternation. On the other wire, string pearl beads and seed beads in alternation.

3. After you've strung all the bicone beads, string pearl and seed beads until beads on both wires are the same length. Make necessary adjustments at this point, since beads vary slightly in size, sometimes enough to make a difference.

4. Twist the two strands of wire, forming a spiral. When you're satisfied with the way the necklace looks, pass wires through a bead tip, then a crimp bead. Compress crimp bead. Cut wires, leaving 1-mm ends, and close bead tip over crimp bead.

5. Attach a spring clasp and an adjustable chain closure with jump rings.

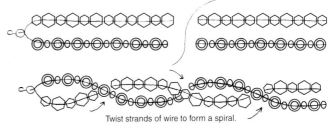

Twist strands of wire to form a spiral.

PEARL AND CRYSTAL FLORAL EARRINGS (shown on pp. 2-3)

	Blue	Pink
20 4-mm Swarovski bicone crystal beads	Montana satin	Rose satin
10 4-mm pearl beads	Metallic blue	Metallic rose
60 2-mm seed beads	Toho 81 (hematite metallic)	Toho 332 (raspberry gold luster)
2 beads equivalent in size to the 3-mm bicone beads (use inexpensive beads, as these will not show), 2 50-cm lengths #3 nylon thread, 2 headpins, ear wires (or earring backs)		

◆Refer to instructions in Steps 1-2 on p. 38.
1. String a bicone bead (starting bead) on center of nylon thread. Designate one end of thread as A, and the other as B. Mark one end with an oil-based marking pen so you can easily distinguish it from the other. Make a check mark in the boxes at left as you complete each step.
   ☐String a seed bead on A.
   Pass B through a seed bead, a pearl bead ①, then a seed bead. Cross A and B over one another with a bicone bead at the intersection.

2. ☐String a seed bead on B.
   Pass B through a seed bead, a pearl bead ②, then a seed bead. Cross A and B over one another with a bicone bead at the intersection.
   ☐String a seed bead on A.
   Pass B through a seed bead, a pearl bead ③, then a seed bead. Cross A and B over one another with a bicone bead at the intersection.
   ☐String a seed bead on B.
   Pass A through a seed bead, a pearl bead ④, then a seed bead. Cross A and B over one another with a bicone bead at the intersection.
   ☐String a seed bead on A. Pass A through starting bead, then a seed bead. String a seed bead on B. Cross A and B over one another with a bicone bead at the intersection.
   You have now completed the central flower (Fig. 2).

◆Continue, referring to Fig. 3.
1. ☐Pass A through a seed bead, a bicone bead ⑤, then a seed bead. String a seed bead on B. Cross A and B over one another with a pearl bead at the intersection.
   ☐String a seed bead on A; pass A through a pearl bead ①, then a seed bead. String a seed bead on B. Cross A and B over one another with a pearl bead at the intersection.

   ☐Pass B through a seed bead, a pearl bead ②, then a seed bead. String a seed bead on A. Cross A and B over one another with a pearl bead at the intersection.
   ☐Pass A through a seed bead, a pearl bead ③, then another seed bead. String a seed bead on B. Cross A and B over one another with a pearl bead at the intersection.
   ☐Pass B through a seed bead, then a pearl bead ④.
   Pass A through a seed bead, a pearl bead ⑤, then a seed bead.

◆Before you tie threads, insert prepared headpin into dome.
2. ☐Insert a headpin into a bead identical in size to a 3-mm bicone bead. Leave the end of headpin longer than usual. Round end (Fig. 4).
   ☐Insert the bead into dome and bring the rounded end out on top of dome. Tie threads together tightly.
   ☐Hide thread ends in 2-3 adjacent beads and cut excess.
   ☐Attach rounded end of headpin to ear wires (or earring backs) (Fig. 5).

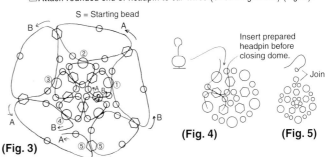

S = Starting bead

Insert prepared headpin before closing dome.

Join.

(Fig. 3)　　(Fig. 4)　　(Fig. 5)

PEARL CHOKER (shown on p. 5)

Finished length: 26cm

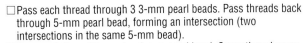

178 3-mm pearl beads	Off-white
104 4-mm pearl beads	Off-white
25 5-mm pearl beads	Off-white
140-cm #3 nylon thread, 2 crimp beads, 2 bead tips, 2 jump rings, clasp, adjustable chain closure	

1. Pass both lengths of nylon thread through a bead tip, then a crimp bead. Compress crimp bead and close bead tip over crimp bead.

Make a check mark in the boxes at left as you complete each step.

2. ☐ Pass both lengths of thread through a 3-mm pearl bead.
   ☐ Pass each of two lengths thread through its own 4-mm pearl bead. Cross A and B over one another with a 3-mm pearl bead at the intersection.

3. ☐ Pass each thread through a 4-mm pearl bead. Cross A and B over one another with a 5-mm pearl bead at the intersection.

☐ Pass each thread through 3 3-mm pearl beads. Pass threads back through 5-mm pearl bead, forming an intersection (two intersections in the same 5-mm bead).

☐ Pass each thread through a 4-mm pearl bead. Cross threads over one another with a 3-mm pearl bead at the intersection.

4. Repeat the pattern described in Step 3 24 more times (total of 25 times).

◆ Work as you did in the beginning.

5. Pass each thread through a 4-mm pearl bead. Pass both threads through a 3-mm pearl bead.

6. Pass both threads through a bead tip, then a crimp bead. Compress crimp bead and close bead tip over crimp bead (see p. 17).

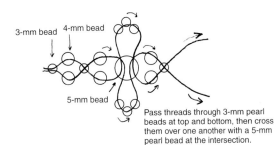

3-mm bead   4-mm bead

5-mm bead

Pass threads through 3-mm pearl beads at top and bottom, then cross them over one another with a 5-mm pearl bead at the intersection.

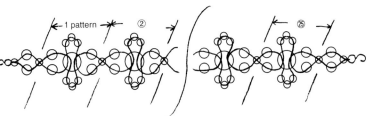

PEARL EARRINGS (shown on p. 5)

14 4-mm pearl beads	Off-white
2 6-mm pearl beads	Off-white
2 30-cm lengths #3 nylon thread, set of 12-mm perforated earring findings for pierced or (non-pierced) ears	

1. String a 6-mm pearl bead (starting bead) on center of nylon thread. Designate one end of thread as A, and the other as B. Mark one end with an oil-based marking pen so you can easily distinguish it from the other.

2. Insert A and B into perforated finding so that the 6-mm bead is situated at its center. Tie A and B together once at back of finding (Fig. 1).

Make a check mark in the boxes at left as you complete each step.

3. ☐ Bring A up through perforated finding to front, and string 7 4-mm pearl beads (①-⑦) on it.
   ☐ Pass A through pearl beads ① and ② (Figure 2).

4. Continue attaching 6-mm pearl bead to finding. Work your way around finding, passing A over nylon thread between pearl beads and through holes in finding. Once you've made a complete round, bring A and B out at back of finding and tie together. Secure knot with glue (Fig. 3)

5. Attach ear wires (or earring backs) to findings.

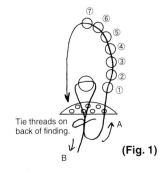

Tie threads on back of finding.

(Fig. 1)

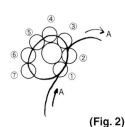

(Fig. 2)

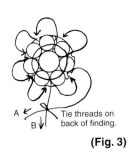

Tie threads on back of finding.

(Fig. 3)

VENETIAN GLASS NECKLACE (shown on p. 8)

Finished length: 36cm

	Blue	Pink
4 6-mm Venetian glass beads	Blue	Pink
3 8-mm Venetian glass beads	Blue	Pink
16 3-mm crackled glass beads	Blue	Pink
2 45-cm lengths nylon-coated wire, 2 crimp beads, 2 bead tips, 2 jump rings, spring clasp, adjustable chain closure		

1. Pass both lengths of wire through a bead tip, then a crimp bead. Compress crimp bead; cut wires, leaving 1-mm ends, and close bead tip over crimp bead (see p. 17).

Make a check mark in the boxes at left as you complete each step.
◆String beads in the following order.
2. ☐String a crackled glass bead on each of two lengths of wire.
   ☐String a 6-mm Venetian glass bead on both lengths of wire.
   ☐String a crackled glass bead on each of two lengths of wire.
   ☐String an 8-mm Venetian glass bead on both lengths of wire.

3. Repeat Step 2 two more times (for a total of 3 times).

4. ☐String a crackled glass bead on each of two lengths of wire.
   ☐String a 6-mm Venetian glass bead on both lengths of wire.
   ☐String a crackled glass bead on each of two lengths of wire.

5. Pass both wires through a bead tip, then a crimp bead. Compress crimp bead where you want necklace to end. Cut wires, leaving 1-mm ends, and close bead tip over crimp bead.

6. Attach a spring clasp to one side of necklace, and an adjustable chain closure to the other with jump rings.

7. Adjust the positions of the Venetian and crackled glass beads to achieve a nice balance. Secure beads with a tiny bit of glue so that they don't shift.

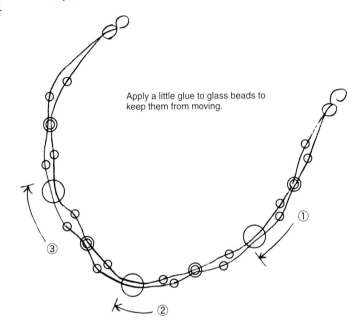

Apply a little glue to glass beads to keep them from moving.

VENETIAN GLASS EARRINGS (shown on p. 9)

	Blue	Pink
2 8-mm Venetian glass beads	Blue	Pink
2 3-mm crackled glass beads	Blue	Pink
2 metallized plastic flower beads	Off-white	Off-white
2 headpins, ear posts (or earring backs)		

1. Insert a headpin into a Venetian glass bead, plastic flower bead, and a crackled glass bead (make two of these).

2. Cut headpin shafts, leaving 7-mm ends. Round ends with round-nose pliers.

3. Attach earrings to posts (or earring backs).

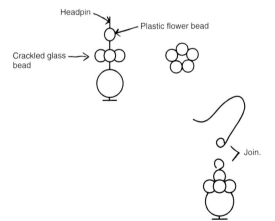

Headpin
Plastic flower bead
Crackled glass bead →
Join.

SNOWFLAKE CHOKER (shown on p. 10)

Finished length: 28cm

	Silver	Crystal
114 4-mm Swarovski bicone crystal beads	Crystal CAL	Crystal AB
248 2-mm seed beads	Toho 29 (silver-lined black diamond)	Toho 21 (silver-lined crystal)
2 100-cm lengths #3 nylon thread, 2 crimp beads, 2 bead tips, 2 jump rings, spring clasp, adjustable chain closure		

◆Since long lengths of nylon thread are hard to work with, we suggest beginning at the center and working outwards.

1. Align 2 lengths nylon thread and tape the center down to your work surface. Designate one end of thread as A, and the other as B. Mark one end with an oil-based marking pen so you can easily distinguish it from the other.

Make a check mark in the boxes at left as you complete each step.

2. ☐String a bicone bead on each of A and B. Cross A and B over one another with a seed bead at the intersection.
☐String a bicone bead, then 3 seed beads on each of A and B. Cross A and B over one another with a bicone bead at the intersection.

3. ☐Pass A through a seed bead, a crystal bead, then a seed bead.
String a seed bead on B. Cross A and B over one another with a bicone bead at the intersection (Fig. 1).
☐Pass A through a seed bead, a bicone bead, then a seed bead.
String a seed bead on B. Cross A and B over one another with a bicone bead at the intersection.
☐Pass B through a seed bead, a bicone bead, then a seed bead.
String a seed bead on A. Cross A and B over one another with a bicone bead at the intersection.
☐Pass A through a seed bead, a bicone bead, then a seed bead.
String a seed bead on B. Cross A and B over one another with a bicone bead at the intersection.
☐Pass B through a seed bead, a bicone bead, then a seed bead.
String a seed bead on A. Cross A and B over one another with a bicone bead at the intersection.
☐Pass A through a seed bead, a bicone bead, then a seed bead.
String a seed bead on B. Cross A and B over one another with a bicone bead at the intersection.
You have completed the snowflake (Fig. 2).

◆Run the thread back through the beads, bringing it out at a (Fig. 3).

(Fig. 1)

a, B, A, Start here, Tape down.

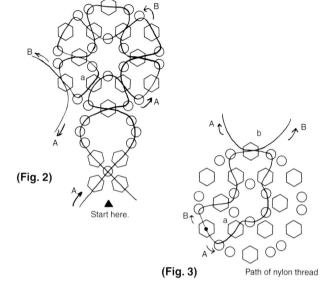

(Fig. 2)

Start here.

(Fig. 3)

Path of nylon thread

4. Referring to Fig. 2, pass thread through beads, crossing them over one another with b at the intersection.

5. ☐String 3 seed beads on each of A and B. Repeat Steps 2-4, making two snowflakes.

6. ☐String 3 seed beads, then a bicone bead on each of A and B. Cross A and B over one another with a seed bead at the intersection.
☐String a bicone bead on each of A and B. Repeat this step 5 more times to make 6 flowers (Fig. 3).

7. String 5 seed beads on each of A and B. String 1 seed bead on both A and B, then a bead tip. You have completed one side of the choker.

◆Remove tape from nylon thread. You will now be working backwards toward other end of choker.

8. String 3 seed beads on A and B. Cross A and B over one another with a bicone bead at the intersection.

9. Repeat Steps 3-5 three times to make 3 snowflakes.

10. End by repeating Steps 6 and 7 (Fig. 4).

11. Attach a spring clasp to one end, and an adjustable chain closure to other with jump rings (see p. 17).

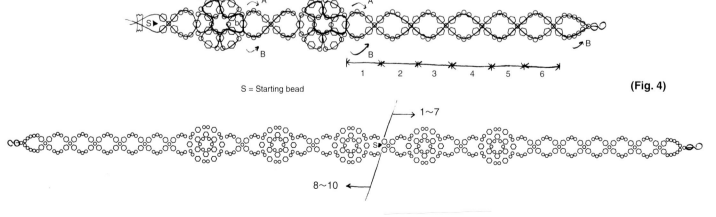

S = Starting bead

(Fig. 4)

1~7

8~10

SNOWFLAKE EARRINGS (shown on p. 10)

	Silver	Crystal
24 4-mm Swarovski bicone crystal beads	Crystal CAL	Crystal AB
36 2-mm seed beads	Toho 29 (silver-lined black diamond)	Toho 21 (silver-lined crystal)
2 60-cm lengths #3 nylon thread, 15-mm perforated earring findings (for pierced or non-pierced ears), glue		

1. String a seed bead, a bicone bead (a), a seed bead, a bicone bead, then another seed bead on center of nylon thread. Designate one end of thread as A, and the other as B. (Mark one end with an oil-based marking pen so you can easily distinguish it from the other.). Cross A and B over one another with a bicone bead at the intersection (Fig. 1).

Make a check mark in the boxes at left as you complete each step.
2. ☐String a seed bead on B.
   Pass A through a seed bead, a bicone bead, then a seed bead. Cross A and B over one another with a bicone bead at the intersection.
   ☐String a seed bead on A.
   Pass B through a seed bead, a bicone bead, then a seed bead. Cross A and B over one another with a bicone bead at the intersection.
   ☐String a seed bead on B.
   Pass A through a seed bead, a bicone bead, then a seed bead. Cross A and B over one another with a bicone bead at the intersection.

☐String a seed bead on A.
   Pass B through a seed bead, a bicone bead, then a seed bead. Form an intersection between A and B in a bicone bead.
☐Pass B through a seed bead, a bicone bead (a), then a seed bead. Pass A through a bicone bead. Form an intersection between A and B in a bicone bead.
   Do not cut the thread. You have completed a snowflake (Fig. 2).

◆Attach snowflake to perforated finding.
3. ☐Place snowflake on top of finding and pass thread through holes in finding.
   Pass A through holes at edge of finding, as though you were stitching a hem.
   ☐When you've made a complete circle, tie threads on back of finding. Secure knot with glue.

4. Attach ear wires (earring backs) to findings.

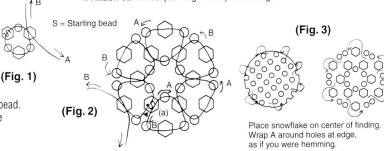

(Fig. 1)

(Fig. 2)

(Fig. 3)

S = Starting bead

Place snowflake on center of finding. Wrap A around holes at edge, as if you were hemming.

CHOKER WITH FLORAL MOTIF (shown on p. 11)

99 4-mm Swarovski bicone crystal beads	Jet hematite
596 2-mm seed beads	Toho 49 (jet black)
2 140-cm lengths #2 nylon thread	
Finished length: 31cm	

1. Pass both lengths of nylon thread through a bead tip, then a crimp bead. Compress crimp bead; cut wires, leaving 1-mm ends, and close bead tip over crimp bead (see p. 17).

Make a check mark in the boxes at left as you complete each step.
2. ☐Pass both lengths of wire through a seed bead.
   ☐String 5 seed beads on each length of wire. Cross lengths of wire over one another with a bicone bead at the intersection (Fig. 1).

3. ☐String 5 seed beads and a bicone bead (① or ②) on each length of wire. Cross A and B over one another with a seed bead (a) at the intersection.

(Fig. 1)

(Fig. 2)

(Fig. 3)

BRACELET WITH FLORAL MOTIF (shown on p. 11)

4-mm Swarovski bicone beads (50)	Jet hematite
2-mm seed beads (210)	Toho 49 (jet black)
2 70-cm lengths #2 nylon thread	
Finished length: 16cm	

☐String a bicone bead (③ or ④), 5 seed beads, a bicone bead, and then 5 seed beads on each length of wire. Cross A and B over one another with a seed bead (a) at the intersection. Then pass them through ① and ②, respectively (Fig. 2).
☐String 5 seed beads on both A and B. Cross A and B over one another with a bicone bead at the intersection (Fig. 3).

4. Repeating Step 3, make 14 flowers (7 for the bracelet) (Fig. 4)

5. String 5 seed beads on each of A and B, then pass both A and B through a seed bead.

6. Pass both ends through a bead tip, then a crimp bead. Compress crimp bead; cut wires, leaving 1-mm ends, and close bead tip over crimp bead.

7. Attach a spring clasp to one end, and an adjustable chain closure to the other with jump rings.

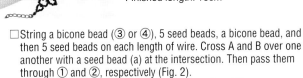

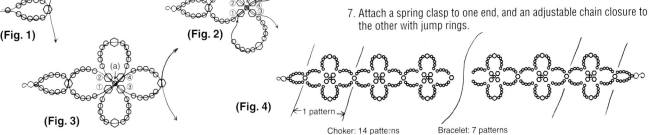

(Fig. 4)

←1 pattern→

Choker: 14 patterns   Bracelet: 7 patterns

FLORAL RING (shown on p. 12)

Finished size: US 6

20 6-mm Swarovski disc crystal beads	Crystal AB
10 2-mm seed beads	Toho 21 (silver-lined crystal)
14 6-mm bugle beads	Toho 21 (silver-lined crystal)
50cm #3 nylon thread	

1. String 4 disc beads (①, ②, ③ and ④) on center of nylon thread. Cross ends over one another with a disc bead at the intersection. Designate one end of thread as A, and the other as B (Fig. 1). Mark one end with an oil-based marking pen so you can easily distinguish it from the other.

Make a check mark in the boxes at left as you complete each step.

2. ☐Pass B through 3 disc beads (⑤, ⑥ and ⑦). Cross A and B over one another with a disc bead at the intersection (Fig. 2).

3. ☐Pass A through 2 disc beads (⑧, ⑨). Pass B through ①. Cross A and B over one another with a disc bead at the intersection.
☐Pass B through 2 disc beads (⑩, ⑪). Pass A through ②. Cross A and B over one another with a disc bead at the intersection.
☐Pass A through 2 disc beads (⑫, ⑬). Pass B through ③. Cross A and B over one another with a bicone bead at the intersection.
☐Pass B through a disc bead (⑭). Pass A through ④ and ⑤. Cross A and B over one another with a bicone bead at the intersection.

◆To strengthen and shape the band, pass thread through beads again, as follows.

4. Pass A through ⑭, ⑬, ⑫ and ⑪.
Pass B through ⑥, ⑦, ⑧ and ⑨.
Cross A and B over one another with ⑩. at the intersection.

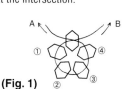

(Fig. 1)

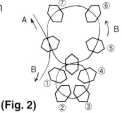

(Fig. 2)

◆Make band (do not cut thread).

5. String a bugle bead on each of A and B. String a seed bead on both A and B without forming an intersection in the seed bead.

6. ☐String bugle beads and seed beads on A and B, one at a time, in alternation. After you've strung the fifth set, pass both A and B through a seed bead without crossing them.

7. ☐String a bugle bead on each of A and B. Pass one end through beads and bring it out at the ★ symbol. Tie And B together twice. Hide thread ends in adjacent beads; cut excess.

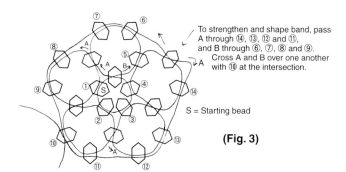

To strengthen and shape band, pass A through ⑭, ⑬, ⑫ and ⑪, and B through ⑥, ⑦, ⑧ and ⑨. Cross A and B over one another with ⑩ at the intersection.

S = Starting bead

(Fig. 3)

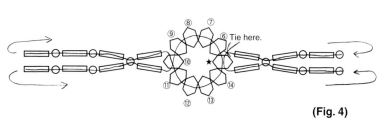

Tie here.

(Fig. 4)

BUGLE BEAD BRACELET (shown on p. 13)

Finished size: 20cm

18 3-mm Swarovski bicone crystal beads	Crystal AB
18 4-mm Swarovski bicone crystal beads	Crystal AB
36 3-mm pearl beads	White
1 6-mm pearl bead	White
210 2-mm seed beads	Toho 21 (silver-lined crystal)
37 6-mm bugle beads	Toho 21 (silver-lined crystal)
4 25-cm lengths #3 nylon thread, 3 jump rings, 2 crimp beads, 2 bead tips, headpin, spring clasp, adjustable chain closure	

1. Pass all 4 lengths nylon thread through a bead tip, then a crimp bead. Compress crimp bead and close bead tip over crimp bead (see p. 17).

2. String beads on 4 lengths of thread (A, B, C and D) as follows.
A: 1 bugle bead, 3 seed beads. Repeat this pattern 16 more times (for a total of 17), then add a bugle bead.
B: 1 bugle bead, 3 seed beads. Repeat this pattern 17 more times (for a total of 18), then add a bugle bead.
C: 3 seed beads, 1 3-mm pearl bead, 1 3-mm bicone bead, 1 3-mm pearl bead, 3 seed beads, 1 4-mm bicone bead. Repeat this pattern 7 more times (for a total of 8), then add 3 seed beads.

D: 3 seed beads, 1 4-mm bicone bead, 3 seed beads, 1 3-mm pearl bead, 1 3-mm bicone bead, 1 3-mm pearl bead. Repeat this pattern 7 more times (for a total of 8), then add 3 seed beads. When you've strung all the beads on one length, tape the end down so the beads won't come off.

3. Pass all 4 lengths of thread through a bead tip, then a crimp bead. Compress crimp bead and close bead tip over crimp bead. Attach a spring clasp to one end, and an adjustable chain closure to the other with jump rings (see p. 17).

4. Insert the 6-mm pearl bead into a headpin. Round end with pliers. Attach headpin to end of adjustable chain closure (cut to about 2cm).

DISK BEAD NECKLACE (shown on p. 12)

Finished length: 37cm

30 6-mm Swarovski disc beads	Crystal AB
18 3-mm Swarovski bicone beads	Crystal AB
18 4-mm Swarovski bicone beads	Crystal AB
36 3-mm pearl beads	White
210 seed beads	Toho 21 (silver-lined crystal)
36 6-mm bugle beads	Toho 21 (silver-lined crystal)

50cm #3 nylon thread, 2 50-cm lengths nylon-coated wire, 2 crimp beads, 2 bead tips, 2 jump rings, spring clasp, adjustable chain closure

1. Follow Steps 1-3 of instructions for the ring on p. 44.

Make a check mark in the boxes at left as you complete each step.

2. ☐Pass A through 2 disc beads (⑮, ⑯). Pass B through ⑥. Cross A and B over one another with a disc bead at the intersection (Fig. 2).
☐String a disc bead ⑰ on B. Pass A through ⑦ and ⑧. Cross A and B over one another with a disc bead at the intersection.
☐String a disc bead ⑱ on A. Pass B through ⑨ and ⑩. Cross A and B over one another with a disc bead at the intersection.
☐String a disc bead ⑲ on B. Pass A through ⑪ and ⑫). Cross A and B over one another with a disc bead at the intersection.
☐Pass B through ⑬, ⑭ and ⑮. Cross A and B over one another with a disc bead ⑳ at the intersection.

3. Pass A through ⑯ and ⑰, and B through ⑲ and ⑧. Tie A and B together twice. Pass ends through adjacent beads; cut excess.

◆Make necklace.

4. Pass both lengths of wire through a bead tip, then a crimp bead. Compress crimp bead. Cut wire, leaving 1-mm ends; close bead tip over crimp bead (see p. 17).

5. String beads on 2 lengths wire, referring to Fig. 3.

6. ☐Pass each of A and B through a bugle bead, a seed bead, then 5 bugle beads. Pass both A and B through a seed bead without crossing them over one another.
☐Repeat instructions in Step 4. Attach clasp to one end and adjustable chain closure to other with jump rings.

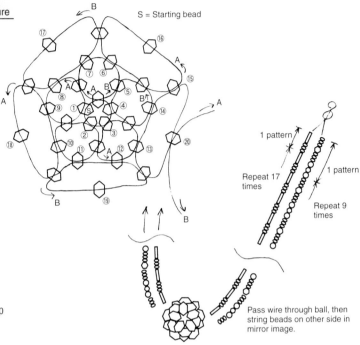

S = Starting bead

1 pattern
Repeat 17 times
1 pattern
Repeat 9 times

Pass wire through ball, then string beads on other side in mirror image.

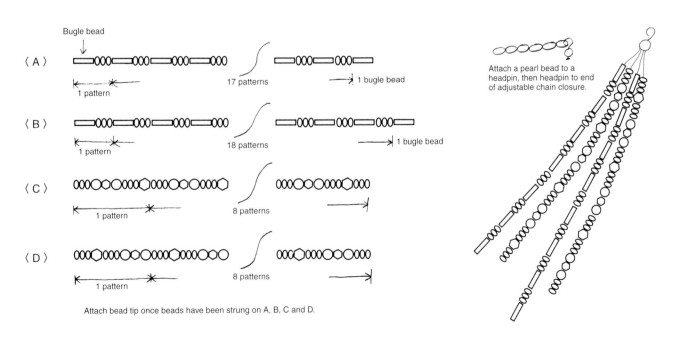

Bugle bead

〈A〉 1 pattern   17 patterns   1 bugle bead

〈B〉 1 pattern   18 patterns   1 bugle bead

〈C〉 1 pattern   8 patterns

〈D〉 1 pattern   8 patterns

Attach bead tip once beads have been strung on A, B, C and D.

Attach a pearl bead to a headpin, then headpin to end of adjustable chain closure.

ANTIQUE GOLD RING (shown on p. 14)

Finished size: US 6

4-mm Swarovski bicone crystal beads	(a) 10 lime
	(b) 5 peridot satin
	(c) 11 light Colorado topaz satin
5-mm Swarovski bicone crystal beads	10 Dorado 2X
108 2-mm seed beads	Toho 221 (bronze metallic)
80cm #3 nylon thread	

1. String a bicone bead (a) on center of nylon thread. This is your starting bead. Designate one end of thread as A, and the other as B (Fig. 1). Mark one end with an oil-based marking pen so you can easily distinguish it from the other.

Make a check mark in the boxes at left as you complete each step.
☐ String a seed bead on A.
☐ Pass B through a bicone bead ① (b) and a seed bead. Cross A and B over one another with a bicone bead (a) at the intersection.

2. ☐ String a seed bead on B.
  Pass B through a seed bead, a bicone bead ② (b), then a seed bead. Cross A and B over one another with a bicone bead (a) at the intersection.
☐ String a seed bead on A.
  Pass B through a seed bead, a bicone bead ③ (b), then a seed bead. Cross A and B over one another with a bicone bead (a) at the intersection.
☐ String a seed bead on B.
  Pass A through a seed bead, a bicone bead ④ (b), then a seed bead. Cross A and B over one another with a bicone bead (a) at the intersection.
☐ Pass A through a seed bead, the starting bead, and another seed bead. Pass B through a seed bead. Cross A and B over one another with a bicone bead (b) at the intersection.
  You have completed the central flower (Fig. 2).

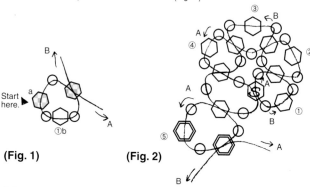

(Fig. 1) **(Fig. 2)**

◆ Continue, referring to Fig. 3.

3. ☐ Pass A through a seed bead, a 5-mm bicone bead ⑤, then a seed bead. Pass B through a seed bead. Cross A and B over one another with a 5-mm bicone bead at the intersection.
☐ Pass B through a seed bead a bicone bead ⑥ (a), then a seed bead. Pass A through a seed bead.
  Cross A and B over one another with a 5-mm bicone bead at the intersection.
☐ Pass B through a seed bead, a bicone bead ①, then a seed bead. Pass A through a seed bead.
  Cross A and B over one another with a bicone bead at the intersection.
☐ Pass B through a seed bead, a bicone bead ⑦, then a seed bead. Pass A through a seed bead.
  Cross A and B over one another with a 5-mm bicone bead at the intersection.
☐ Pass B through a seed bead, a bicone bead ②, then a seed bead. Pass A through a seed bead.
  Cross A and B over one another with a 5-mm bicone bead at the intersection.

☐ Pass B through a seed bead, a bicone bead ⑧ (a), then a seed bead. Pass A through a seed bead. Cross A and B over one another with a 5-mm bicone bead at the intersection.
☐ Pass B through a seed bead, a bicone bead ③, then a seed bead. Pass A through a seed bead.
  Cross A and B over one another with a 5-mm bicone bead at the intersection.
☐ Pass B through a seed bead, a bicone bead ⑨, then a seed bead. Pass A through a seed bead.
  Cross A and B over one another with a 5-mm bicone bead at the intersection.
☐ Pass B through a seed bead, a bicone bead ④, then a seed bead. Pass A through a seed bead.
  Cross A and B over one another with a 5-mm bicone bead at the intersection.
☐ Pass A through a seed bead, a 5-mm bicone bead ⑤, then a seed bead. Pass B through a seed bead. Cross A and B over one another with a bicone bead (a) at the intersection.

◆ Work around the perimeter of the dome, inserting 2 seed beads between bicone beads.

4. ☐ Pass B through 2 seed beads, a bicone bead ⑥, 2 seed beads, a bicone bead ⑦, 2 seed beads, a bicone bead ⑧, 2 seed beads and a bicone bead ⑨. Cross A and B over one another with 2 seed beads at the intersection.
  You have completed the floral dome.

S = Starting bead

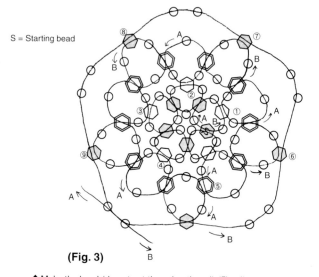

(Fig. 3)

◆ Make the band (do not cut the nylon thread) (Fig. 4).

5. Pass A and B (now extending from the dome) through 2 seed beads. Cross A and B over one another with a bicone bead (c) at the intersection. Repeat this pattern 11 times. The 12th time, do not cross A and B over one another. Instead, pass them through to the ★ symbol and then tie them twice. Run thread ends through adjacent beads and cut excess.

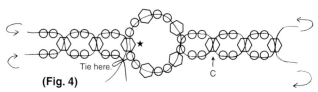

Tie here.

(Fig. 4) C

ANTIQUE GOLD NECKLACE (shown on p. 14)

78 3-mm Swarovski bicone crystal beads
20 4-mm Swarovski bicone crystal beads

10 5-mm Swarovski bicone beads
160 2-mm seed beads
70cm #3 nylon thread, 50cm nylon-coated wire, 2 crimp beads,
2 bead tips, 2 jump rings, spring clasp, adjustable chain closure

Light Colorado topaz satin
(a) 10 lime
(b) 10 peridot satin
Dorado 2X
Toho 221 (bronze metallic)

Make a dome, following Steps 1-3 of instructions for ring on p. 46.

◆Close back of dome (Fig. 4).
Make a check mark in the boxes at left as you complete each step.

4. ☐Pass A through a seed bead, a bicone bead ⑩ (b), then a seed bead.
   Pass B through a seed bead. Cross A and B over one another with a bicone bead (b) at the intersection.
   ☐Pass A through a seed bead, a bicone bead ⑥, then a seed bead.
   Pass B through a seed bead. Cross A and B over one another with a bicone bead (b) at the intersection.
   ☐Pass B through a seed bead, a bicone bead ⑦, then a seed bead.
   Pass A through a seed bead. Cross A and B over one another with a bicone bead (b) at the intersection.
   ☐Pass A through a seed bead, a bicone bead ⑧, then a seed bead.
   Pass B through a seed bead. Cross A and B over one another with a bicone bead (b) at the intersection.
   ☐Pass B through a seed bead, a bicone bead ⑨, a seed bead, and a bicone bead ⑩. Cross A and B over one another with a seed bead at the intersection.
   You have completed a miniature rose.

5. Run A through the beads on the perimeter until it reaches B (both should be facing in the same direction). Tie A and B together twice. Hide ends in 2-3 nearby beads; cut excess.

◆Make necklace (Fig. 5).
1. String a bead tip, then a crimp bead on one end of the wire. Compress crimp bead. Cut wire, leaving a 1-mm end. Close bead tip over crimp bead (see p. 17).

2. String 2 seed beads and 2 3-mm bicone beads on wire. Repeat this pattern 38 times (for a total of 39). Add 2 more seed beads.

3. Insert wire into the 3 seed beads on back of miniature rose (indicated by ☆ symbol in Fig. 6). Run it through nylon thread on back of rose, and bring it out at opposite side (Fig. 6). The rose will look the same on both sides, but it's best to designate the side where you cut the nylon thread as the back.

4. Pass wire through 2 seed beads and 2 3-mm bicone beads. Repeat this pattern 38 times (for a total of 39). Add 2 more seed beads, a bead tip and a crimp bead. Compress crimp bead, cut wire, and close bead tip over crimp bead.

5. Attach a spring clasp to one end, and an adjustable chain closure to the other with jump rings.

Back view

(Fig. 6)

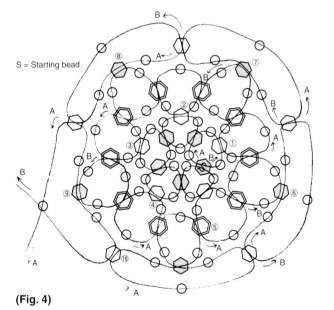

S = Starting bead

(Fig. 4)

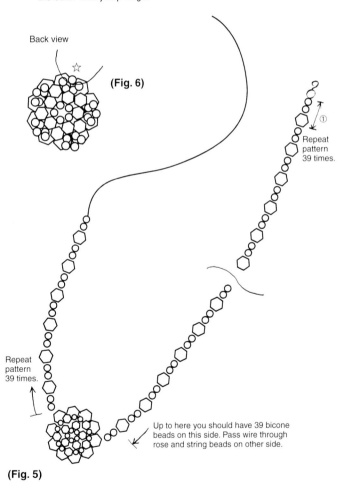

Repeat pattern 39 times.

Repeat pattern 39 times.

Up to here you should have 39 bicone beads on this side. Pass wire through rose and string beads on other side.

(Fig. 5)

◆See p. 21 for instructions.

ANTIQUE GOLD SLAVE RING (shown on p. 14)   Finished size: US 6

36 4-mm Swarovski bicone crystal beads	12 lime	12 peridot satin	12 light Colorado satin
154 2-mm seed beads	Toho 221 (bronze metallic)		
80cm #3 nylon thread			

■Color charts for Slave Ring

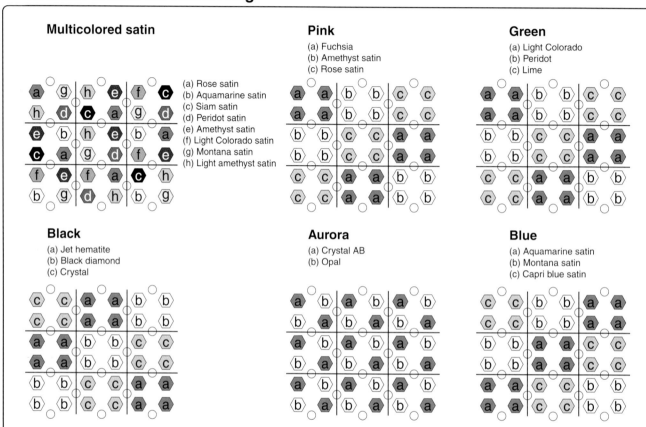

Multicolored satin

(a) Rose satin
(b) Aquamarine satin
(c) Siam satin
(d) Peridot satin
(e) Amethyst satin
(f) Light Colorado satin
(g) Montana satin
(h) Light amethyst satin

Pink
(a) Fuchsia
(b) Amethyst satin
(c) Rose satin

Green
(a) Light Colorado
(b) Peridot
(c) Lime

Black
(a) Jet hematite
(b) Black diamond
(c) Crystal

Aurora
(a) Crystal AB
(b) Opal

Blue
(a) Aquamarine satin
(b) Montana satin
(c) Capri blue satin

■Color charts for Duet Ring

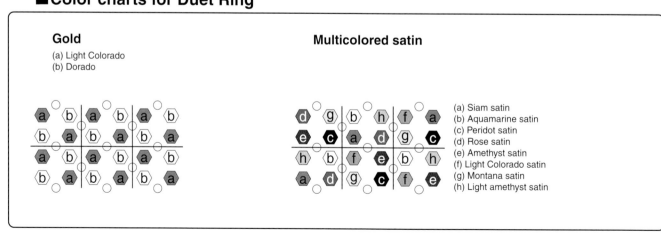

Gold
(a) Light Colorado
(b) Dorado

Multicolored satin

(a) Siam satin
(b) Aquamarine satin
(c) Peridot satin
(d) Rose satin
(e) Amethyst satin
(f) Light Colorado satin
(g) Montana satin
(h) Light amethyst satin

Eyeglass chain (A)	Gold	Silver
12 4-mm Swarovski bicone crystal beads	Topaz	Green tourmaline
12 4-mm Swarovski round crystal beads	Olivine	Peridot
6 6-mm Swarovski bicone crystal beads	Light Colorado topaz	Chrysolite
12 2-mm seed beads	Toho 22 (Silver-lined amber)	Toho 172 (greenish-yellow)
30 eyepins	Gold	Rhodium
50cm chain	Gold	Rhodium
2 0.8 x 5-mm jump rings, 2 eyeglass holders		

Eyeglass chain (B)	Black	Silver
20 4-mm Swarovski round crystal beads	Jet	Crystal
8 6-mm Swarovski round crystal beads	Jet	Crystal
2 3-mm seed beads	Toho 81 (hematite metallic)	Toho 21 (silver-lined crystal)
20 eyepins	Black	Rhodium
4 headpins (0.5 x 20mm)	Black	Rhodium
60cm chain	Black	Rhodium
2 0.8 x 5-mm jump rings, 2 eyeglass holders		

Eyeglass chain (A)

1. Cut four 2.5-cm lengths of chain. Set aside remainder of chain, which will be used to form center of eyeglass chain.

2. Insert an eyepin into each crystal bead. Cut eyepin shafts, leaving 7-mm ends; round ends.

3. Join beads attached to eyepins in this order: 4-mm bicone bead, 4-mm round bead, 6-mm bicone bead, 4-mm round bead, 4-mm bicone bead. Make six of these groups (three for each side of eyeglass chain).

4. Attach each group of beads to a 2.5-cm length of chain. Use two lengths of chain to join three groups. Repeat for other side of eyeglass chain.

5. Join components made in Step 4 with remaining chain to form center of eyeglass chain. Cut chain to desired lengths.

6. Attach eyeglass holders with jump rings.

Eyeglass chain (B)

1. Cut four 2.5-cm lengths of chain. Set aside remainder of chain, which will be used to form center of eyeglass chain.

◆Make flowers with 2 headpins.

Make a check mark in the boxes at left as you complete each step.

2. ☐Insert a headpin into a 4-mm round bead, a seed bead (a), then a 4-mm round bead. Bend headpin gently, referring to Fig. [figures not labeled]. Cut pin shaft, leaving a 7-mm end. Round end.
   ☐Insert another headpin into a 4-mm round bead, the same seed bead (a) as before, then a 4-mm round bead. Bend headpin gently, then cut shaft, leaving a 7-mm end. Round end.
   Make another identical flower.

3. ☐Insert eyepins into remaining beads and round ends.
   ☐Join beads now attached to eyepins in this order. 4-mm round bead, 6-mm round bead, 4-mm round bead. Make another identical group.

4. ☐Referring to drawings, join beads as follows: 6-mm round bead, 4-mm round bead, flower made in Step 2, 4-mm round bead, 6-mm round bead. Make another identical group.

5. Referring to drawings, join groups made in Steps 3 and 4 with chain. Use chain set aside in Step 1 for center section, first cutting it to desired length. Attach eyeglass holders with jump rings.

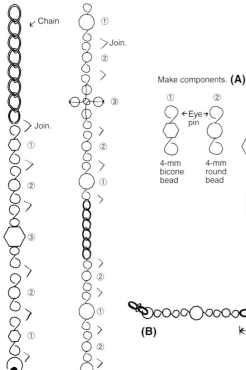

Make components. **(A)**

① ← Eye → pin
4-mm bicone bead

② 4-mm round bead

③ ← Eyepin
← Seed bead
6-mm bicone bead

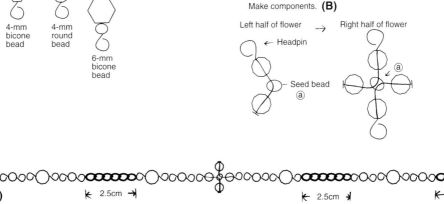

Make components. **(B)**

Left half of flower → Right half of flower

← Headpin
← Seed bead (a)
(a)

(B)
2.5cm   2.5cm   40cm
Join opposite side in same way.

(A)
Chain 2.5cm   2.5cm   32cm
Join opposite side in same way.

Wave Choker

This choker, which shimmers in the sunlight, has a very modern look.

Instructions are on p. 52.

Dark Purple Red Silver

Choker with Leather Cord

The matte leather cord and sparkling crystal motifs make for a winning combination.

Instructions are on p. 53.

Purple Pink Blue Orange Green

WAVE CHOKER (shown on p. 50)

Finished length: 30cm

	Purple	Pink	Silver
105 4-mm fire-polished beads	Iris red	Aurora red	Mirror
101 2-mm seed or 3-cut beads	Toho 356 (magenta-lined crystal luster 3-cut beads)	Toho 356 (magenta-lined crystal luster 3-cut beads)	Toho 29 (silver-lined black diamond seed beads)
2 60-cm lengths #3 nylon thread, 2 crimp beads, 2 bead tips, 2 jump rings, spring clasp, adjustable chain closure			

1. Designate one end of nylon thread as A, and the other as B. Mark one end with an oil-based marking pen so you can easily distinguish it from the other. Align two strands of thread and pass them through a bead tip, then a crimp bead. Compress crimp bead, cut thread, leaving a 1-mm end. Close bead tip over crimp bead (see p. 17).

2. String a fire-polished bead on each of A and B. Cross A and B over one another with a seed bead at the intersection (Fig. 1).

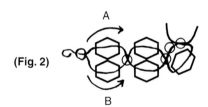

(Fig. 1)

Make a check mark in the boxes at left as you complete each step.

3. ☐ String a fire-polished bead on each of A and B. Cross A and B over one another with a seed bead at the intersection.
   ☐ String a seed bead on A, and a fire-polished bead on B. Cross A and B over one another with a seed bead at the intersection (Fig. 2).
   ☐ String a fire-polished bead on each of A and B. Cross A and B over one another with a seed bead at the intersection.
   ☐ String a fire-polished bead on A, and a seed bead on B. Cross A and B over one another with a seed bead at the intersection. You have completed one pattern.

4. Repeat the pattern worked in Step 3 15 more times (for a total of 16). You can adjust the length of this choker by adding or subtracting patterns. The choker (without findings) will measure 28cm with 16 patterns.

5. ☐ String a fire-polished bead on each of A and B. Cross A and B over one another with a seed bead at the intersection.
   ☐ String a seed bead on A, and a fire-polished bead on B. Cross A and B over one another with a seed bead at the intersection.
   ☐ String a fire-polished bead on each of A and B. Cross A and B over one another with a seed bead at the intersection.
   ☐ String a fire-polished bead on each of A and B.

There are many types of Czech beads, including faceted beads, designer beads and lamp beads. The beads used to make this choker are called "fire-polished beads." The names and product numbers of these beads differ from store to store, so ask before you buy.

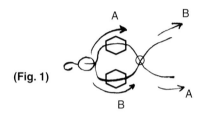

(Fig. 2)

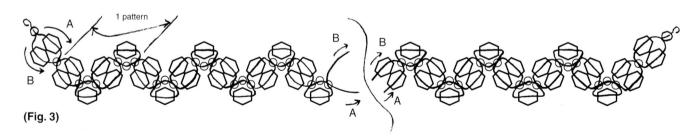

(Fig. 3)

CHOKER WITH LEATHER CORD (shown on p. 51)

Finished length: 20cm

	Orange	Blue	Violet	Pink	Green
15 6-mm Swarovski bicone crystal beads	Hyacinth	Montana	Amethyst	Fuchsia	Light Colorado topaz
64 4-mm faceted Czech fire-polished beads	Light Colorado rose	Light sapphire	Mirror violet	Mirror rose quartz	Olive
138 2-mm seed beads	Toho 221 (bronze metallic)	Toho 248 (Black-lined dark blue rainbow)	Toho 607 (3-cut beads)	Toho 221 (bronze metallic)	Toho 221 (bronze metallic)
2 30-cm lengths leather cord	Rust	Blue	Purple	Rust	Brown
140cm #3 nylon thread, 2 0.8 x 5-mm jump rings					

1. String 15 seed beads on center of nylon thread. Cross ends over one another with a seed bead at the intersection.

2. String a fire-polished bead on both each of two lengths of thread.

Make a check mark in the boxes at left as you complete each step.

3. ☐ String a fire-polished bead on each of two threads. Cross ends over one another with a bicone bead at the intersection.
☐ String 3 seed beads on both left and right threads. Pass threads back through bicone bead, forming an intersection.

4. Repeat this pattern 14 times (for a total of 15). To lengthen or shorten the choker, add or subtract patterns. If you work 15 patterns, you should end up with a choker that is 20cm long (minus the leather cord).

◆ Repeat beginning sequence.

5. ☐ String a fire-polished bead on each of two lengths of thread. Cross ends over one another with a seed bead at the intersection.
☐ String 15 seed beads on one length of thread. Tie threads together twice. Run ends through a few adjacent beads; cut excess.

◆ Attach leather cord.

6. ☐ Thread leather cord through seed bead loops at each end. Fold cord over (1-2cm).
☐ Open jump ring and thread it onto cord (where cord is folded over). Close jump ring with flat-nose pliers (see photographs).
☐ Close jump rings tightly (see photographs below).

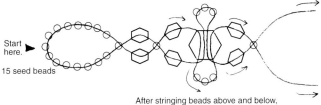

Start here.
15 seed beads

After stringing beads above and below, cross ends over one another with a bicone bead at the intersection.

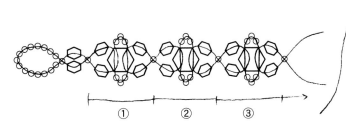

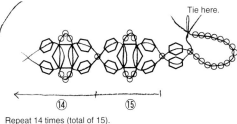

Tie here.

① ② ③

⑭ ⑮

Repeat 14 times (total of 15).

◆ Closing a jump ring

1. Open the jump ring, and pass cord (leather cord in photograph) through it. Grasp both sides of jump ring with flat-nose pliers.

2. Squeeze the pliers hard so the cord won't slip out.

3. Rotate cord several times as you compress it with pliers. When you're finished, jump ring should look like the one in the photo.

Cell Phone Straps

Don't be surprised if all your friends want one of these.

Blue Pink Yellow Crystal Purple

Strap with heart center   Instructions are on p. 56.

Pink Purple Blue Green

Strap with heart dangle   Instructions are on p. 57.

Purple Green Blue Pink

Strap with clover dangle   Instructions are on p. 57.

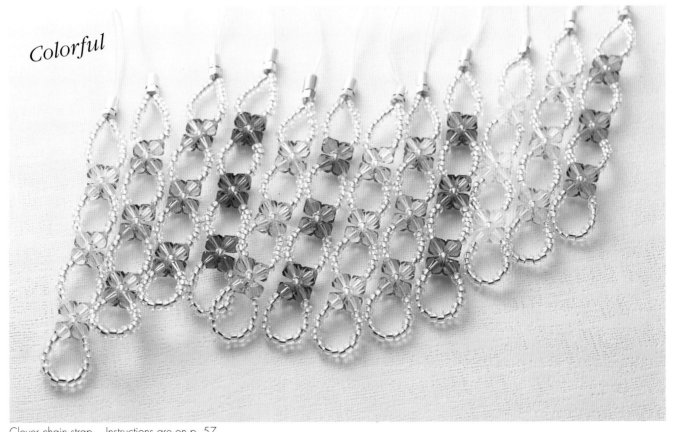

Colorful

Clover chain strap   Instructions are on p. 57.

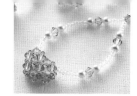

STRAP WITH HEART CENTER (shown on p. 54)   Finished length: 10cm

	Pink	Blue	Purple	Yellow	Crystal
24 6-mm Swarovski bicone crystal beads	Light rose	Aquamarine	Violet	Jonquil	Crystal
8 5-mm Swarovski pearl beads	Cream rose	Cream rose	Cream rose	Cream rose	Cream rose
16 3-mm seed beads (for heart)	Toho 38 (silver-lined bright pink)	Toho 104 (aqua transparent luster)	Toho 1300 (neodymium)	Miyuki H54 (yellow)	Toho 1
43 3-mm seed beads (for strap)	Toho 1 (crystal transparent)	Toho 1 (crystal transparent)	Toho 1	Toho 1	Toho 1
80cm #3 nylon thread, 30cm #8 nylon thread, crimp bead, strap finding					

Make a check mark in the boxes at left as you complete each step.

1. ☐For the heart center, string two 3-mm seed beads on center of an 80-cm length #3 nylon thread. Designate one end of thread as A, and the other as B. Mark one end with an oil-based marking pen so you can easily distinguish it from the other.
   ☐String a bicone bead on each of A and B. Cross A and B over one another with 2 seed beads at the intersection.

2. ☐Repeat Step 1 (Row 1) until you have worked 7 rows. Row 8: Close the circle by passing A through a bicone bead, then through the 2 seed beads at starting point. Cross A and B over one another with a bicone bead at the intersection (Fig. 1).

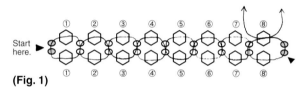

(Fig. 1)

◆Arrange the piece so that ①-⑧ are at the top.
3. Add 2 bicone beads (⑨ and ⑩) (Fig. 2).
   ☐String a bicone bead ⑨ on B.
   ☐Pass B through ①.

4. ☐Cross A and B over one another with a bicone bead ⑩ at the intersection (Fig. 3).
   ☐Pass A through ②; pass B through ④. Cross A and B over one another with ③ at the intersection.
   ☐Pass A through a seed bead (a); pass B through a seed bead (b). Bring A and B out on back of piece.

5. Work back of heart in the same way as the front, adding 2 bicone beads (⑨' and ⑩').
   ☐Cross A and B (now emerging from a and b) over one another with ③' at the intersection.
   ☐Pass A through ②'; pass B through ④'. Cross A and B over one another with ⑩' at the intersection.
   ☐Pass A through ⑨'; pass B through ①'. Cross A and B over one another with ⑧' at the intersection.

6. ☐Pass A through a seed bead (d) (Fig. 5).
   Pass B through ⑦',⑥', ⑤' and ⑨', then a seed bead (c).
   Now A and B are on the front of the heart.

7. ☐Pass B (extending from seed bead (c)) through ⑦, ⑥, ⑤, ⑨ and ⑧. Tie B to A (extending from seed bead d) twice. Hide thread ends in adjacent beads; cut excess (Fig. 6).

8. ☐String beads on 30cm #8 nylon thread, referring to Fig. 7.
   ☐Pass thread through top of heart, then continue stringing beads. Pass both lengths of thread through a seed bead, then the bottom of strap finding.
   ☐Pass threads through a crimp bead. Compress crimp bead. Cut threads, leaving 1-mm ends. Attach top of strap finding.

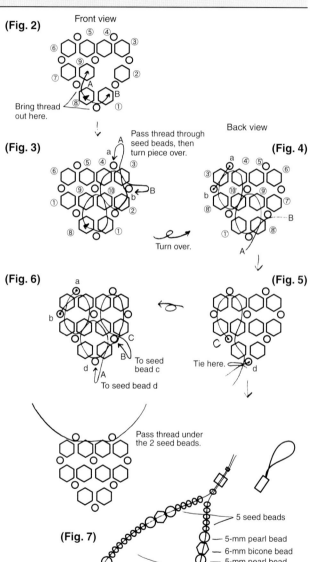

(Fig. 2) Front view

(Fig. 3) Pass thread through seed beads, then turn piece over.

Bring thread out here.

Turn over.

(Fig. 4) Back view

(Fig. 5) Tie here.

(Fig. 6) To seed bead c / To seed bead d

(Fig. 7)

Pass thread under the 2 seed beads.

- 5 seed beads
- 5-mm pearl bead
- 6-mm bicone bead
- 5-mm pearl bead
- 8 seed beads
- 8 seed beads

STRAP WITH CLOVER DANGLE (shown on pp. 54-55)   Finished size: 10cm

Strap with clover dangle	Pink	Blue	Purple	Green
6 6-mm Swarovski bicone crystal beads	2 rose 4 light rose	2 Montana 4 light sapphire	2 amethyst 4 light amethyst	2 emerald 4 peridot
12 5-mm pearl beads	White	White	White	White
53 3-mm seed beads	Toho 21 (Silver-lined crystal)	Toho 21 (Silver-lined crystal)	Toho 21 (Silver-lined crystal)	Toho 21 (Silver-lined crystal)
35cm #8 nylon thread, crimp bead, 1.2 x 7-mm jump ring, strap finding, clover dangle				

Strap with heart dangle	Pink	Blue	Purple	Green
6 6-mm Swarovski bicone crystal beads	Rose	Light sapphire	Amethyst	Peridot
12 5-mm pearl beads	White	White	White	White
53 3-mm seed beads	Toho 21 (Silver-lined crystal)	Toho 21 (Silver-lined crystal)	Toho 21 (Silver-lined crystal)	Toho 21 (Silver-lined crystal)
35cm #8 nylon thread, crimp bead, 1.2 x 7-mm jump ring, strap finding, heart dangle				

1. String 10 seed beads on the center of nylon thread.

2. On each side of thread string a pearl bead, a bicone bead, a pearl bead, 8 seed beads, a pearl bead, a bicone bead, a pearl bead, 8 seed beads, a pearl bead, a bicone bead, a pearl bead and 5 seed beads.

Make a check mark in the boxes at left as you complete each step.
3. ☐ Pass both thread ends through a seed bead.
   ☐ Pass both thread ends through bottom of strap finding and a crimp bead. Compress crimp bead right near bottom of strap.
   ☐ Cut excess thread and attach top of strap finding.

4. Attach heart (or clover) dangle at center of first 10 seed beads strung with a jump ring.

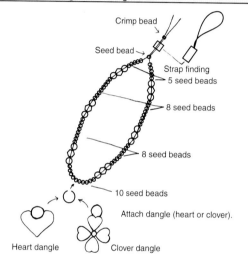

Crimp bead
Seed bead →
Strap finding
5 seed beads
8 seed beads
8 seed beads
10 seed beads
Attach dangle (heart or clover).
Heart dangle
Clover dangle

CLOVER CHAIN STRAP (shown on p. 55)   Finished length: 10cm

6-mm Swarovski bicone crystal beads	12 chrysolite 12 tanzanite	12 peridot 12 aquamarine	12 rose 12 light sapphire	12 fuchsia 12 sapphire	12 violet 12 white opal	12 jonquil 12 topaz
70 3-mm seed beads	Toho 21 (silver-lined crystal)	Toho 21	Toho 21	Toho 21	Toho 21	Toho 21
35cm #8 nylon thread, crimp bead, strap finding						

1. String 18 seed beads on center of nylon thread.

2. String a bicone bead on each side of thread.
   Pass both thread ends through a seed bead, then string a bicone bead on each length of thread.
   You have completed the crystal bead flower. Make sure not to form an intersection in a seed bead, since doing so will alter the design.

3. String 7 seed beads on each length of thread. Make two more flowers by repeating Step 2 twice, for a total of three.

Make a check mark in the boxes at left as you complete each step.
4. ☐ String 10 seed beads on each thread end.
   ☐ Pass both thread ends through a seed bead.
   ☐ String bottom of strap finding and a crimp bead on both thread ends. Compress crimp bead right near bottom of finding.
   ☐ Cut excess thread; attach top of finding.

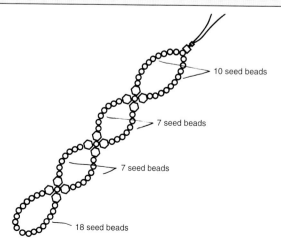

10 seed beads
7 seed beads
7 seed beads
18 seed beads

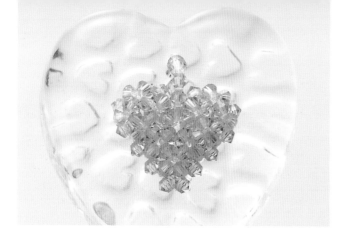

How to make the heart center

Our favorite heart design is made from 81 Swarovski crystal beads. We have attempted to make the instructions as clear as possible. (Instructions for the Heart Necklace are on p. 60.)

1

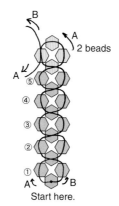

1. Begin by making one side of the heart. The pink crystal bead will form one shoulder of the heart.

Make a check mark in the boxes at left as you complete each step.

☐ String a bicone bead on center of thread. Designate one end of thread as A, and the other as B.

☐ String a bicone bead (①) on each of A and B. Cross A and B over one another with a bicone bead at the intersection. Repeat four times (②-⑤).

☐ String 2 bicone beads on A. Cross A and B over one another with a bicone bead at the intersection.

2

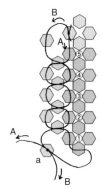

2. You can now see the beginnings of a three-dimensional shape. Keep thread tight so that heart keeps the proper shape.

☐ Pass A through ⑤, and B through a bicone bead. Cross A and B over one another with a bicone bead at the intersection.

☐ Repeat until you reach ②.

☐ Pass A through ① and starting bead. Cross A and B over one another with a bicone bead (a) at the intersection.

3

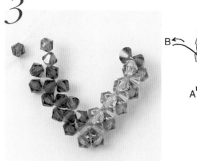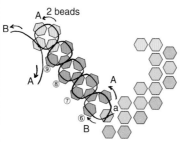

3. Make other side of heart.

☐ String a bicone bead on each of A and B. Cross A and B over one another with a bicone bead at the intersection.

☐ Repeat three times (⑦-⑨). Pass A through 2 bicone beads. Cross A and B over one another with a bicone bead at the intersection.

4

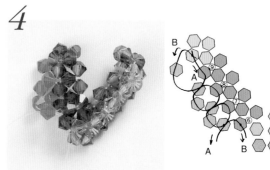

4. Now the heart shape is clearly defined.

☐ Pass A through ⑨, and B through a bicone bead. Cross A and B over one another with a bicone bead at the intersection.

☐ Repeat until you reach ⑦.

☐ Pass B through ⑥; turn piece over.

5

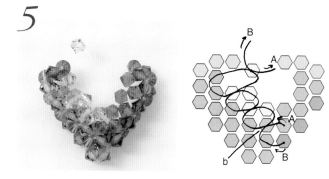

5. Form front of heart.

Make sure thread extends from bead shown in drawing at left.

☐ Pass B through adjacent bead. Cross A and B over one another with a bicone bead (b) at the intersection.

☐ Pass A through adjacent bead, and B through a bicone bead. Cross A and B over one another with a bicone bead at the intersection.

☐ Pass B through adjacent bead, and A through a bicone bead. Cross A and B over one another with a bicone bead at the intersection.

☐ Pass A through 2 adjacent beads (see drawing). Cross A and B over one another with a bicone bead at the intersection.

6

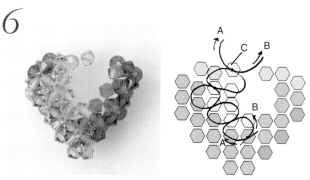

6. When you reach top of heart, turn piece over.

☐ Pass B through adjacent bead, and A through a bicone bead. Cross A and B over one another with a bicone bead (c) at the intersection. When you look at the heart from the top, you'll see that (c) is located right between the front and back (in the center). Turn piece over as soon as you complete the intersection in (c).

Top view

7

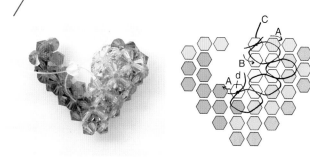

7. Add more bicone beads, working toward bottom of heart.

☐ Pass A through adjacent bead, and B through a bicone bead. Cross A and B over one another with a bicone bead at the intersection.

☐ Pass B through 2 adjacent beads. Cross A and B over one another with a bicone bead at the intersection.

☐ Pass A through adjacent bead, and B through a bicone bead. Cross A and B over one another with a bicone bead at the intersection.

☐ Pass B through 2 adjacent beads. Cross A and B over one another with a bicone bead (d) at the intersection.

8

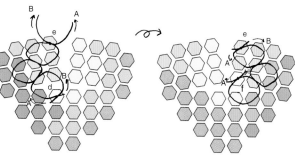

8. Add more beads, this time working toward top of heart. Turn piece over when you reach the top.

☐ Pass A through adjacent bead, and B through a bicone bead. Cross A and B over one another with a bicone bead at the intersection.

☐ Pass B through 2 adjacent beads. Cross A and B over one another with a bicone bead at the intersection.

☐ Pass A through adjacent bead, and B through a bicone bead. Cross A and B over one another with a bicone bead (e) at the intersection. Like (c), (e) should be situated at top center of heart.

9

9. Add beads to fill in center of heart. Pass thread ends through bicone beads, and bring them out at same location.

☐ Turn piece over when thread end extends from (e).

☐ Pass B through adjacent bead, and A through a bicone bead. Cross A and B over one another with a bicone bead at the intersection.

☐ Pass A through 2 adjacent beads. Cross A and B over one another with a bicone bead at the intersection.

☐ Pass B through 2 adjacent beads. Cross A and B over one another with a bicone bead (f) at the intersection.

HEART NECKLACE (shown on p. 6)

Finished length: 36cm

	Pink	Pale pink	White	Blue	Light blue
145 3-mm Swarovski bicone crystal beads	Fuchsia	Light rose	Crystal AB	Light sapphire	Light Azore
130 2-mm seed beads	Toho 356 (magenta-lined crystal)	Toho 38 (silver-lined bright pink)	Toho 161 (crystal rainbow)	Toho 168 (Light sapphire transparent rainbow)	Toho 170 (blue topaz dyed rainbow)
110cm #3 nylon thread, 45cm nylon-coated wire, 2 bead tips, 2 crimp beads, 2 jump rings, clasp, adjustable chain closure					

10

(Continued from p. 59)
10. Form a loop from thread ends.
   □ Pass B (extending from f) through g, h and i.
   □ Pass A through j, k and l.
   □ Pass both A and B through 9 bicone beads.

   Close on opposite side.
11. □ Pass one end of thread through m and n, and the other through o and p.
   Tie A and B together twice. Hide ends in adjacent beads; cut excess.

◆ Make necklace.
12. □ String a bead tip and crimp bead on one end of wire. Compress crimp bead; close bead tip over crimp bead.
   □ String 2 seed beads and 1 bicone bead on wire in alternation. Finish with a bead tip and crimp bead.

13. □ Pass necklace through heart. Attach a spring clasp to one end and an adjustable chain closure to the other with jump rings.

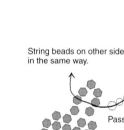

String beads on other side in the same way.

69 bicone beads
140 seed beads

Pass necklace through heart.

HEART RING (shown on p. 7)

Finished size: US 6

	Pink	Pale pink	White	Blue	Light blue
47 4-mm Swarovski bicone crystal beads	Fuchsia	Light rose	Crystal AB	Light sapphire	Light Azore
52 2-mm seed beads	Toho 356 (magenta-lined crystal luster 3-cut beads)	Toho 38 (silver-lined bright pink)	Toho 161 (crystal rainbow)	Toho 168 (light sapphire transparent rainbow)	Toho 170 (blue topaz dyed rainbow)
70cm #3 nylon thread					

◆ Make heart first.
Make a check mark in the boxes at left as you complete each step.
1. □ String a bicone bead on center of thread. Designate one end of thread as A, and the other as B.
   □ String a bicone bead (①) on each of A and B. Cross A and B over one another with a bicone bead at the intersection. Repeat twice (②-③). String 2 bicone beads on A. Cross A and B over one another with a bicone bead at the intersection.

2. □ Pass A through ③, and B through a bicone bead. Cross A and B over one another with a bicone bead at the intersection.
   □ Repeat with ②.
   □ Pass A through ① and starting bead. Cross A and B over one another with a bicone bead (a) at the intersection.

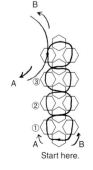

Start here.

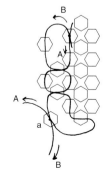

3. ☐String a bicone bead on each of A and B. Cross A and B over one another with a bicone bead at the intersection. Repeat one more time.
☐Pass A through 2 bicone beads. Cross A and B over one another with a bicone bead at the intersection.

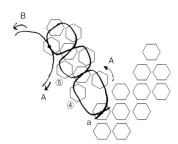

4. ☐Pass A through ⑤, and B through a bicone bead. Cross A and B over one another with a bicone bead at the intersection.
☐Pass B through ④.

Make sure that thread extends from location shown in drawing.
5. ☐Pass B through adjacent bead. Cross A and B over one another with a bicone bead (b) at the intersection.
☐Pass A through adjacent bead.

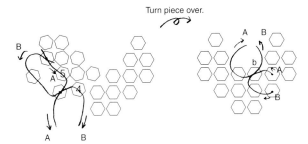

Turn piece over.

6. ☐String a bicone bead on B. Cross A and B over one another with a bicone bead at the intersection.
☐Pass B through 2 adjacent beads (see drawing).

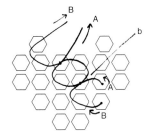

7. ☐Cross A and B over one another with a bicone bead (c) at the intersection.
When you look at the heart from above, you'll see that (c) is located between front and back (in the center). Turn piece over once you've made the intersection in (c).

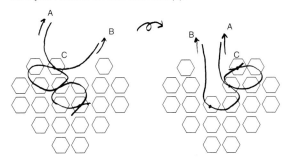

8. ☐Pass A through 2 adjacent beads. Cross A and B over one another with a bicone bead at the intersection.
☐Pass B through 2 adjacent beads.

Make sure that thread extends from location shown in drawing.
9. ☐Cross A and B over one another with a bicone bead at the intersection.
☐Pass A through 2 adjacent beads. Cross A and B over one another with a bicone bead (d) at the intersection.
Turn piece over with thread extending from (d).

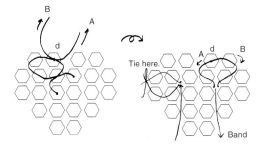

◆Make band.
10. ☐Pass A through adjacent bead, and B through 2 adjacent beads. Make sure that thread extends from location shown in drawing.

11. ☐String 2 seed beads on each of A and B. Cross A and B over one another with a bicone bead at the intersection.
☐Repeat 12 times (for a total of 13). Make adjustments in size, if necessary, by adding or subtracting repetitions.
☐Pass thread ends from locations shown in drawing through 2 adjacent beads. Tie A and B together twice. Hide ends in adjacent beads; cut excess.

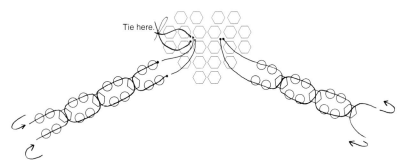

BEAD FANTASIES : Beautiful, Easy-to-Make Jewelry
by Takako Samejima

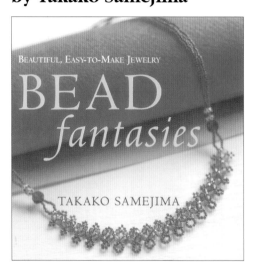

Color photographs of 10 of the 71 pieces include necklaces, bracelets, rings, earrings, brooches, hair ornaments, cell phone straps and eyeglass chains. 66 pages are devoted to brief instructions for the jewelry, supplemented by small color photographs and detailed color drawings. On the last few pages are supplies, and some lessons covering basic bed-stringing, weaving and finishing techniques.

84 pages: 7 1/8 x 7 1/8 in., paperback US$18.00
ISBN: 4-88996-128-3 EAN:978-4-88996-128-7

BEAD FANTASIES II : More Beautiful, Easy-to-Make Jewelry
by Takako Samejima

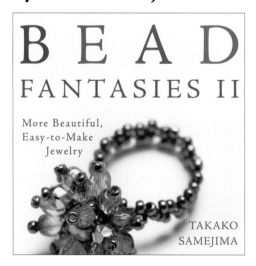

With beautiful color photos, detailed drawings and step-by-step instructions, renowned jewelry designer Takako Samejima makes it easy for even the beginner to create eye-catching, original bead accessories. Bead Fantasies II is divided into three sections. The first part focuses on different accessories designed around one motif, for example a clover, a Diamond-shaped flower, a crown. The second section offers patterns that allow readers to use their own beads to create completely original pieces. The third part, entitled "Bead Items" is organized by type of accessory-rings, earrings, bracelets, necklaces and brooches.

84 pages: 7 1/8 x 7 1/8 in, paperback US$18.00
ISBN: 4-88996-188-7 EAN: 978-4-88996-188-1

BEADS AND WIRE : Jewelry and Decorative Items for the Home

Featuring over 55 projects to be made freehand or with a wire-working tool, magnificent color photos, detailed instructions and descriptions of findings and other essential supplies. Beads and Wire is the perfect book for beginners to this craft, aficionados, or anyone wanting to create exquisite jewelry and elegant home accessories.
64 pages: 8 1/4 x 10 in., 100 color photos, paperback US$17.95
ISBN: 4-88996-114-3   EAN: 978-4-88996-114-X

ANTIQUE STYLE BEAD ACCESSORIES

by matsuko Sawanobori

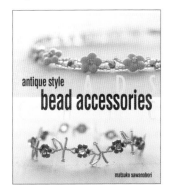

Includes both classic and contemporary fashions while providing detailed instructions for making rings, necklaces, chokers, pins, hair ornaments, amulet bags and more.
72 pages: 7 1/2 x 8 1/2 in., 56 color pages, 16 illustrations, paperback US$15.95
ISBN: 4-88996-089-9   EAN: 978-4-88996-089-1

BEADER'S PALETTE

With examples of designs both daring and refined, This book shows how beads of standard sizes and shapes can be combined in dramatic way. With detailed drawings, complete introductions and material guide, it's the perfect guide to learning to make dozens of wearable accessories.
96 pages: 8 1/4 x 10 1/8 in., 46 full color pages, 32 illstations, .paperback US$19.00
ISBN: 4-88996-097-X EAN: 978-4-88996-097-6